MORCOTT

Cover Art by Artist Langley Fox Hemingway.

Logo design by Breanna Lam. Indian Ink.

ISBN: 979-8-9921767-0-4

First Edition 2024.

WWW.MORCOTTMATERIAL.COM

A THOUSAND THOUGHTS
FOOD FOR THE SOUL

"Enlightenment is as simple as seeing the light of which you are each a part."

MORCOTT

INTRODUCTION

Tamsin began these pages upon a trip to Peru and we have assisted her in scribing them upon her travels between Peru, France, Spain, Ireland and England as well as her 'home country,' the United States of America.

Tamsin is a member of our family, in a sense, but she too is human. She will be assisting us for her human existence, in this form, upon this plane, in order to speak our words.

Tamsin was born in England and was raised by parents from England and America and now resides in the Southern California region.

She was created for the purpose of scribing these words and we are grateful for her volunteering and for her contributions of many kinds, including her work as a scribe and speaker for the Morcott Material and the Lumerian sector of the Galactic Federation.

Tamsin is tailor-made for the job of speaking and scribing for the Lumerians as a hybrid of sorts herself. She wrote these words for us between the years 2021 and 2023. She has also been working on a third book which is soon to be released in the later months of 2025

In this book we will give one thousand inspirations as reminders to you all of that which you of course already know. We will continue with volume three in 2025 and will release more than thirty books in Tamsin's lifetime (through her.)

We intend to build foundations with these first three books upon which we will teach more sophisticated principles for living upon this plane, and with which you may co-create at your optimum the worlds in which you live and that you affect. 'The All.'

We look forward to sharing this journey with you and hope you enjoy these thousand 'thoughts.'

- Introduction by Morcott, in confluence with Tamsin, the Oracle of Morcott.

NOTE FROM MORCOTT

May these words soothe and ignite your soul and may you each do unwaveringly that which you feel to upon a soul level.

1

Existence is a journey, take each step with this in mind. Do not expect to understand your destination, for there is forever a new step to take and we cannot fathom it until it is taken.

2

You are each a part of all else that is.

~

3

When you take time to do as you feel you are able to access the wisdom of the All.

4

Take your time to do as you feel each day,
in each moment even. By simply doing as you
feel on a soul level you will find staircases and
doorways appear to you in the precise
timing that suits you best.

~

5

Take time to do as you feel and you will find
your life will unfold in a display of miracles.

6

You are one with all things at all times.
Your understanding of this is the most
profound experience available on this,
or any seemingly 'other,' plane.

~

7

Choose carefully that which you say and
that which you do. In each moment of your
existence you hold all the powers
of the Universe.

8

Do for others as you wish for them to do for ye. Since you are one, you are serving one and all by being kind to your kindred man.

~

9

By simply doing as you feel, you are changing all that is, for all time.

10

You are a collaborative part of all that is,
creating all that is.

~

11

Take your time to do as you feel, and all will
unfold as perfectly as a flower in the sun.

12

Since time doesn't really exist,
you may take as much of it as you like.

~

13

With all your being,
give that which you feel.

14

Do as thy feel and that which you wish to do
will come unto you with ease and clarity.

~

15

Each and every being upon
this planet belongs.

16

Since you each belong, you each are kindred.

~

17

In each moment know that you are all that is.

18

Becoming one is only achieved by becoming oneself, one and all.

~

19

Take only what feels correct, give unto others that which you feel.

20

With each step give and receiveth grace.

~

21

Take your time to contemplate that which
you already know.

22

We are all one at all times, there is nothing
separate from any other thing,
ever.

~

23

Peace comes to those who know that they are
at one with all beings.

24

You are now and have always been an
irremovable part of the Universe.
We could not exist without you.

~

25

The absolute truth is O. (One/ Oneness/
complete/ whole/ All- 'nothingness.')

26

All cannot exist without each one,
one cannot exist without the All.

~

27

Do as thy feel and all that you wish for will
come to you with ease.

28

What is it you came here to do? Once
you have established this, put all of your force
into its creation. With each step, ask yourself/
the All if you are on course. There is nothing
more important to do.

~

29

In deciding what it is you will spend
your life doing, or even this week for that
matter, you will need to first consider what
it is you have to offer the All in its journey
of wholistic expansion. You each have a
cherished gift to offer.

30

That which you have been granted,
is your gift to give.

~

31

Do not be afraid to do as you feel, it truly is
the very most important thing to do.

32

Surround yourselves with that which
you wish to be a part of, for there are no
boundaries and all are one.

~

33

Oneness is the truth of all being.

34

Wonder upon these lands and know that you are at one with all that is, that this world is not alone in its existence.

~

35

We will always be at one with all that is.

36

Together we will know ourselves as 'individuals,' and as one. You cannot understand yourself without understanding the All. You cannot understand the All without understanding yourself.

~

37

Worrying is creating that which you do not wish for. Listen to and adhere by that which

38

With each step remember your oneness with
all that is. Feel the earth beneath your feet of
which you are a part. Caress the waters that
too are a part of you. Know that you are one
with all things, and 'love' all that is.

~

39

Without question, do as you feel on a soul
level. Your mind is, in more cases than not, a
hinderance to the knowings of your soul.

40

By taking the time to listen to, and honor
yourself, you are doing so for all others,
both directly and indirectly.
You are all that is.
We all are.

~

41

Begin in this, and in every moment,
to be here now.

42

There is nowhere to be but the present.

~

43

In each moment, consider what feels
integrally important or appropriate.
Do only this, always.

44

By taking time to be present, one creates
time to be powerful in that which
they came here to do.

~

45

By listening to oneself one may listen
to the All.

46

You are all 'all powerful' for you are all one.
We are all 'all powerful,' for we are all one.

~

47

Exist here. Now. All the 'time.'

48

Begin in this moment to find presence.
Ultimately you will understand that you are
at one with all things. The things you love,
the things you think you detest, and all else
in between. There is nothing you are not.

~

49

Upon this realm there are many ways by
which one may serve the All (and indeed
oneself as all are one). Do as thy feel upon
a soul level. We design what is possible
with each thought and each action.

50

Manifestation is merely the way by which the Universe expands. It is not specific to wealth, relationships or promotions, it is that which you create as your world with every thought, feeling and action. You are all creating all the time. Do so with care and grace.

~

51

By listening to oneself, one is able to listen to the All.

52

Since we are all one,
one is honoring oneself by honoring others.

~

53

Treat all with respect and presence of spirit
and all will be at your fingertips.

54

In all worlds there is peace. It can be found at
the center of one's soul.

~

55

Come together and find your
oneness with all that is.

56

United you are not only stronger but you
hold the powers of all in existence.

~

57

If you are in pain, breathe into it and know
that each ailment was invited unto oneself
for profound reason.

58

You know all that is, for you are all that is.

~

59

Behave as one and all shall be in harmony.

60

Serve only all that is and all shall be well.

~

61

Becoming one is becoming yourself.

62

Selflessness too, is self-care.

~

63

By simply being, one has the profound ability
to do whatever it is they feel, for one has
found trust in all that is.

64

Be thyself and find the whole.
It has always been there, as have you.

~

65

By becoming one, we are becoming oneself.

66

All worlds are one. All beings are one.
All that is, is one. There is nothing that
you are not.

~

67

Everything you see and everything you do
not see that is in existence, exists as a part of
you, and you as a part of it.
There is no division.
There is only all.

68

By simply taking the time to do as you feel,
you will find yourself on course.

~

69

Treasure each moment for there is nothing
else in existence but that which is now.

70

Love and respect all beings, including yourself.
You are all as sacred as one another.

~

71

There is nothing in this multiverse that is
not a part of you.

72

We are all, all that is.

~

73

Existence is merely an experience to expand
the greater self.

74

All beings are one. All are one being.

~

75

There is nothing in this multiverse that you are not.

76

Anxiousness is a gift. It helps direct you to
that which needs to be shifted, discarded,
or absorbed. Listen to thyself.

~

77

Take the time each day to consider what you
feel to do. One can save a lot of time
by doing nothing.

78

Do nothing often.

~

79

None of you are not a part of the All.

80

Be kind to yourself.
You are 'God.'

~

81

Everything that you can see, that apparently
surrounds you, is in fact a part of you.

82

By loving yourself, you are loving others.
By loving others, you are loving yourself.
With both in place, balance may be found.

~

83

By making choices that resonate on a soul
level, you will find that the opportunities in
your life alter.

84

By choosing to do that which feels integrally
correct, you will find that everything you
need will flow to you with greater ease.

~

85

Peaceful will thee be when thy knowst
all is all there is.

86

All there is, is all there is.

~

87

By choosing to do as one feels upon a soul level, one undertakes all that is.

88

Listen to what you feel, not to that which you think. Balance comes to those who tune in to their soul's calling. By focusing not upon thought, balance may be found.

~

89

Taking the time to do as you feel is honoring yourself and the All.

90

By emptying your mind of all that fills it,
through you flows the Universe.

~

91

Quieten your mind and allow
your light to grow.

92

Take the time to step correctly,
for each step creates the road that you tread.

~

93

Your children are gifts from the Universe.
They are brighter than the stars that stud
your skies and as malleable as the water of
your world. Be sure to take the time to be
present with each one of them. They are you,
and they are the All. Teach them not what you
think but what you feel. Change comes when
old ideas are let go of. Do not fear change,
nor enforce it. Do as thy feel.

94

In every moment all is in transition. Bring
what you have to give unto this world. Do
not be afraid and do not doubt your ability.
You are 'all powerful'. You are all that is.
You are all one.

~

95

If you are seeking still what your gift is to
share with this world, you have only to listen
to your heart; within it lie the secrets, and the
answers and the wholeness of all that is, and
within it lies your truth. You are the gift.

96

Truth comes in many forms,
yet it always resonates as one.

~

97

Do as you feel, and that which unfolds
will be your chosen path.

98

Do not be afraid. Fearing anything, even a total illusion, will only add to the power of that which you react to. I stress, choose what it is you wish to focus your energies upon.

~

99

Black and white do not exist.
All are one.

100

Taking steps in the direction of one's soul's calling will always result in one's perfect path.

~

101

Love all those whom surround you in any given situation and one will find they too feel loved. Since we are all one, that which we create in grace, we essentially benefit from.

102

We are all one, always.
We were never separate and will never be.

~

103

This world is going through a great
transition and your work is imperative. Do as
you feel upon a soul level. Your soul's journey
'here' may be different to that which you have
told yourself, or have been told by others.
Always simply do as you feel.

104

By telling others that which you love
and appreciate about them, you create more
of such virtues within the All.

~

105

Be kind always, regardless of how you have
been treated. Great change is created when
one does as one feels.

106

Loving yourself is loving the All.

~

107

Take the time to do as you feel, and your world will be as you wish it to be.

108

By truly listening to oneself and to the All
one may save much apparent time.

~

109

Do as thy feel, always.

110

By listening to oneself one is able to be
at one with the All.

~

111

Love is all there is.

112

Everything you do, say, feel, think affects
everything there is. Live with precision.

~

113

May each step you take upon this plane be in
accordance with your soul's calling.

114

Breathe in that which you wish.

~

115

Speak only that which is worthy of sharing.
Speak intuitively. Live intuitively.

116

By listening to oneself, one may hear the All.

~

117

Kindness is a gift for both the giver
and the receiver.

118

Listen to the breath of the wind, it speaks
to you of great wisdoms.

~

119

Breathe in the All and know your oneness.

120

Oneness is you.

~

121

Oneness is the collision of all the beauty of this multiverse. We have always been one, we are now merging to a concentration that has not been in place before.

122

Do as you feel, and all will become as you
and the All intended.

~

123

Truth is that which resonates upon
a soul level.

124

Be upon this plane, it is where you have
chosen to be. You will leave precisely when
is right for you and the All.

~

125

Take your time to consider what it is you
wish for, it may be quite different to that
which you imagine on anything less than
a soul level.

126

Be here now, there is nowhere else to be.

~

127

Listen to what it is your heart is telling you,
do not allow your thoughts to quieten
the callings of your soul.

128

Love those around you, for they are all that is.

~

129

Do precisely as you feel, you are your own
guide, and each have many assisting them
on their path.

130

By listening to that which you feel,
you may access the wisdom of the All,
it flows through each of you.

~

131

What is it you wish to do?
Listen to thyself.

132

Look not externally for the answers,
for they lie within you.

~

133

Your body speaks to you.
What does it say?

134

Since we are all essentially one,
one must listen to oneself in order to know
what's best for the All.

~

135

You are each equipped with the wisdom of all
else that is, let it flow through you like a river
to the ocean. You are too the ocean.
We are all the All.

136

By taking the time to simply be, one may save
many lifetimes of exploration.
Your soul speaks softly.
What does it say?

~

137

Breathe in to your mind's eye,
it will illuminate all that you see.

138

Consider carefully what feels correct
and what does not. You know, always.

~

139

All beings are blessings. Be kind to, and
appreciative of, those whom you come across.
If someone is unkind to you, turn darkness
into light by choosing kindness in return.

140

We are all here to make a difference.
We are all doing what we came here to do.
In order to live in this realm at your optimum,
simply do as you feel to do upon a soul level.

~

141

You have been equipped with all the tools
needed to do as you came here to do.

142

Listen to your heart's calling,
it wishes for the wellness of the All.

~

143

By simply being, in all circumstances,
one allows for the opportunity to be a
part of the All in 'live time.' To enact from
a place of presence, simply do as you feel in
each moment. The Universe is changing in
every moment, therefore the very best way
to lend to the optimization of all that is, is by
simply being yourself, by simply doing,
saying and being what you feel.

144

You are each as a jigsaw piece, and the
puzzle cannot be complete without each and
every one of you. When each piece is entirely
itself the puzzle is no longer a puzzle but a
perfect painting of all that that is,
at its shining optimum.

~

145

All in existence is relative to perception.

146

That which surrounds you is a part of you.

~

147

Take the time to consider your oneness
with the All, and all will change.

148

Listen to that which surrounds you,
we each breathe the same breath.

~

149

Know your oneness with the All.
It is all that is.

150

By understanding your oneness with all that
is, one realizes that nothing is not oneself and
that everything is oneself and that therefore
oneself does not exist, or that
oneself is all there is.

~

151

Breathe in the All in each breath.

152

Pain may be diverted by one's understanding
in the temporal solidity upon this realm.
We are all with you and can assist you in
carrying your burdens upon this plane by
your simple recognition of this truth.

~

153

Loneliness does not exist in reality,
for we are all one. Remember this
when the opposite appears to be true.
Appearances can indeed be deceiving.

154

Nobody truly possesses anyone or anything.
Trust. You are all beings, and you are all that is.

~

155

Challenges come only to those whom are
ready for the lesson at hand. Do not doubt
your ability to do something simply because
you have not done it before.

156

Focusing upon the breath is the quickest route
to finding one's oneness within the All.

~

157

Take time each day to simply focus
upon one's breath, no such time will be
wasted. By allowing oneself time for this
focus, one allows the Universe within them
and that they are amidst, to expand
with every breath.

158

By focusing upon the energetic centers
that exist within each of you one is able to
listen to the Universe as it speaks,
for it is within you.

~

159

You are as solid as everything else in your
world. Solidity is validated only by perception.

160

Choose to breathe with the wind.
You are one with all things.

~

161

Since solidity is essentially an 'illusion,'
one might consider what else one wishes to
lend their energies to creating.

162

Since all are one, there is only one eye that
sees. This is something not to be afraid of,
but to tap in to. It belongs to you all.

~

163

Darkness and light are essentially one.
All are one. We are all.

164

By considering that which one is
hesitant to acknowledge within oneself,
one is most able to accept difficulties in
other's behavior and to forgive and embrace.
Be kind to all beings, including yourself.

~

165

If you are finding it challenging to know what
it is that your heart says then take the time to
be quiet, to sit or to walk in nature and listen
to the All, of which you are a part.

166

Much 'magic' can happen in a very short
period of your apparent time.

~

167

Time is an illusion which each and every
one of you have the ability to surpass.

168

There is no such thing as death. Remember
who you are. It is not merely the vessel within
which you sit or stand. You are the All and
you may play any part you wish.

~

169

Nourish yourself with that which your body
calls for. Be aware of illusion within
this process. Listen to thyself.

170

'Addiction' is one's lack of commitment to
the present moment. Identify what it is that
you are wishing to avoid and take the time to
work through these principles:

Why did I come here?
What do I wish to do?
Need I forgive myself or others?
Where do I feel to be and with whom?
What is it I am afraid of, or am I avoiding?
All is well my child. Do not be afraid.

~

171

By simply listening to one's own needs,
one is in part tending to the needs of the All.
Do not doubt your own power, it is immense.

172

Kindness is a gift that one
benefits from embracing.

~

173

Forgiveness, though often challenging,
is one of the most effective ways of embracing
the light of which you are each made.

174

Forgiving others helps you to be fully yourself
and forgiving yourself allows others to
be whole in your presence.

~

175

Hope is at times useful and during others
destructive. Intuition, inner light, knowingness
is most effective. Choose to be present
to that which you know.

176

No matter how strange or illogical an
act may seem, if you feel upon a soul level to
do it, then do so with grace. Choose only that
which essentially serves you and all others.

~

177

You cannot fully honor another without
also honoring yourself.

178

Each of you have the ability to see with your
soul. Listen to your heart and note that which
is real beyond this realm.

~

179

There truly is nothing to worry about, ever.
If a challenge persists that cannot be avoided,
then worrying will aid this. If the challenge
may be avoided, then one's energies are best
invested by focusing upon this truth.

180

Do as you feel, not as you think or have been
told, unless these align with your soul's calling.

~

181

Trust in yourself.
You hold the powers and the wisdom of
all that is.

182

Though all is changing, you will always be
a part of it, as you have always been.
We cannot exist without you,
for you are each the All.

~

183

There is nothing to fear.
All that is, is not only at your side,
but also within you.

184

The Universe is a part of you, and you are a part of the Universe. Nothing is separate and no one is ever alone.

~

185

Beauty is all that is. You need not compete; this will only result in sadness. Instead, choose to see beauty in all things and it will radiate from you as you reflect unto yourself that which you behold. How fortunate we each are.

186

Beyond this realm you will find reflections of
the All, everything replicates and reflects upon
itself. All is familiar for all is one. Nothing is
truly strange. Everything is kindred.

~

187

Forgiveness is one of man's most powerful
tools. Use it generously.

188

Forgiveness is a way by which one can
transform darkness into light, 'hate' into love
and foe into brethren. Always respect oneself
and all others. Always be kind to oneself and
all others. Do not expect the same in response.
Know that by behaving as such, the All will
reflect this unto you in one
form or another.

~

189

Do not despair if that which you wished for
has turned into dust. You wished for this also,
what blessings might it hold?

190

If you long for another, then listen to what
it is you wish for of yourself. Honor yourself
and trust the All for you have created your
journey as such for great reason.

~

191

Do not be afraid, all is always well and
precisely as you all, in unison,
designed it to be.

192

Decide things with your heart, not with your mind. Your mind is a useful tool, use it carefully and do not let it influence you beyond what your heart says is true.

~

193

Be yourself and you will allow those whom you commune with to be as they too feel to be.

97

194

Quieten your mind so that
your heart may be heard.

~

195

Choose your company with care and
intuition. You do not need to honor another
by spending time with them if you wish to
be alone. In fact, by honoring yourself in
this way you allow the other space to evolve.
Remember to always be kind.

196

Taking the time to thank others for that
which has served you will result in both
parties benefitting. Gratitude is a most
powerful and abundant gift or tool,
use it earnestly and often.

~

197

Listen to your soul,
it speaks in wisdoms.

198

Family is always chosen.
Why might you have chosen this family?

~

199

By simply being, one allows the Universe to
pour through them.

200

When from a place of presence one is gifted
with an idea, be sure to note it.

~

201

Breathe-in grace, it surrounds each
and every one of you.

202

Present yourself as you feel to, do not
conform for the sake of conforming.
Do as thy feel upon a soul level, always.

~

203

Remember that by being yourself, you are
showing others that they may do the same.

204

Listen to others and be present to
what they say. Take on board only that
which resonates upon a soul level. What is
true for each of you may differ in varying
degrees at this stage of 'evolution.'

~

205

Be sure to be kind always.
Kindness grows as you share it. It is one of the
most powerful tools you possess.

206

Be yourself, for you are a bright and beautiful
shining light that will show others the way to
be their true selves. You are each as bright and
as beautiful as all the stars in the Universe.

~

207

Listening to oneself is the very best way
to achieve what you came here to do. You
need not remember your mission in full, you
need only do as you feel upon a soul level.
Follow this path in each step that you take.
You cannot stray, there are many alternate
routes and the journey you design and walk
is always imperative to one's learning.

208

Praying is important, 'literally.'
You may import anything needed from the
All, of which you are all a part.

~

209

Feel not the need to teach others that which
you are in the midst of discovering. Instead,
continue in your discovery. None of you and
all of you are teachers. No one upon this
plane is a true master of the All. Once you
become aware of your oneness, you need not
speak in order to share these wisdoms as you
surpass all planes. All is vibration. You may
share by simply being.

210

Happiness is a gift for the All. Find it,
share it, honor its beauty and reverence.
Do that which makes you truly
happy upon a soul level.

~

211

When one decides to live their life
according to their inner callings, one
realizes that the opportunity to do so was
always there and that life flows more freely
and with more ease, joy and integrity.
Do as thy feel my brethren.

212

Timelessness is always the time.
Do as you feel, always.

~

213

Support others upon their path and you
will find your own is more defined.

214

Take each step in the direction of
your dreams as it avails itself to you.

~

215

Listen to what others speak with their hearts,
not only with their mouths.

216

Trust in oneself for you hold all
the wisdom of the Universe.

~

217

Uni-Versa = One movement, one whole,
one being, one world of many worlds.
All affects all. You are all that is.

218

Presence breeds creativity. One can more powerfully create when one is right here, now.

~

219

All things are 'holy.' Love and respect all things. This includes oneself.

220

Take the steps available and others will
form themselves at your feet.

~

221

Listen to yourself.
You already know the answer.

222

Perform acts of love and compassion as often
as you feel to, each of these change the
world in which you live.

~

223

Kindness is key to happiness.

224

All art your brethren.

~

225

You are all loved, and we shall always
be with each of you.

226

Nature speaks to those who listen.

~

227

Calm your mind and allow all that is to flow through you. You are the All.

228

Seek not others to validate your thoughts,
instead listen to your soul.

~

229

Each of you have the ability to heal
yourselves, be sure to lend your attentions
to this. The power is within you.

230

Listen to your heart, it will tell you which
step is correct.

~

231

Gratitude is a precursor to receiving
all that you wish. Wish only for that of
your soul's resonance.

232

Kindness to others is kindness to self. Since all
are one, one can benefit oneself by doing
as they feel to do for others.

~

233

Oneness is all that is.

234

All living things are 'beings'
and you are all one being.

~

235

Know thy oneness.

236

All are All.

~

237

Listen to yourself and
you will hear the All.

238

Reality is that which you collaboratively create with your thoughts and your actions. You are changing it in every moment.

~

239

Creation is an ability we each have. There is one creator, all of you are that creator. It is not separate from you and could not exist without each and every one of you.

240

Love is innate to all beings.
Love is truly all there is.

~

241

Since we each collaborate in creating our
reality, it is imperative that we each do
as we feel upon a soul level.

242

Reality is merely a projection of
mass creation. It changes in every instant.
What is it you wish to contribute to the All?

~

243

By living as you feel to you are changing the
world, and with it all others.
For all affects the All.

244

Solidity is an interpretation.
As you change, so too does your reality.

~

245

Words are tools with which to create
your reality. Use them wisely.

246

Kindness to others is a way by
which you may serve all that is.

~

247

What can you do right now that would
change your life for the better? Is there
resistance? If so, that is wonderful.
Now you know where to begin.

248

Support one another upon your journeys,
the road is less rocky when one reflects unto
themselves the support one has
given unto 'others.'

~

249

'Meditation' is a way by which you may
speak to the All. It may not speak in words.
Words can be helpful and yet words can also
be limiting. Not all can be expressed by them.
Listen to that which you feel, each day.

250

Have you an ailment?
What might this mean?
Everything is a blessing and a lesson.
Ask oneself: why might I have chosen this?

~

251

You chose the reality in which you were born
and you now exist. This is changing almost
constantly. What are you choosing and why?

252

Do not be unkind to another because they
have 'wronged you' for this cannot rectify
the 'wrongdoing.' Instead, choose to live as
you feel the world could be. Kindness and
compassion are powerful tools of creation.
You each have the power to turn
darkness into light.

~

253

Darkness and light will always exist,
but as we progress, the balance will become
harmonious, and all will be whole in a
state of kindness and calm.

254

Listen to all beings, those who 'speak' and
those who apparently do not. There is much
to learn from all beings.

~

255

Nature is a part of you,
and you are a part of nature.
Nature is the All.

256

You are an irremovable 'part' of all that is
and shall always be. We are eternal.
There is nothing to fear.

~

257

Listen to Love.

258

By trusting in the 'Universe' you are
trusting in oneself, by trusting in oneself
one is trusting in the 'Universe,'
for all are one.

~

259

The truth lies within you because you are
the All. You hold all within you and you are a
'part' of all that perceivably surrounds you.
In fact, if this may be fathomable to you:
you are all, all of all that is.

260

There is no true separation
between anything whatsoever.

~

261

It is an energetic 'rule' that that which
you present unto all that is, is essentially that
which you receive in return. For all 'reflects'
all. Be sure to contribute that which
you feel to upon a soul level.

262

By simply listening to oneself, one may save
themselves a great deal of your imagined
'time.' Do as thy feel, always.

~

263

Each step in the direction of your
soul's calling upon the plane will be
taken not only by you but shared with
all others as a blessing to each of you.
Thank you for your contribution.

264

If you feel lost take the time to be in nature
for it will show you what it is you need to see.

~

265

Miracles come in many forms.
You are each a miracle.

266

Everything you know to be 'true' is
reenforcing a reality of 'live creation.' Choose
carefully what you lend your energies to.
You are all creating the All.

~

267

God is all that is.

268

There is nothing that is not 'God.'

~

269

God is not separate from you, it is you.
All of you, and all that is.

270

By living your life in the way that you truly
wish, you are doing your part to save the
world and all others with it.

~

271

Listen to thyself for you are the All
and hold within you the entire
Universe and that beyond.

272

Do not be afraid. Fear begets fear.
Love begets love.
Choose wisely.

~

273

With each challenge that arises ask oneself
"why might I have chosen this?"
You are the dictator of your own dreams.

274

All is beauty.
All is one.

~

275

As a child one knows innately,
if not consciously, what it is they came here
to do. In many, or most cases, this is dissuaded
from them whilst they are still young.
Re-find your soul's calling by simply listening
to yourself. Take each step that you feel to
upon a soul level. These steps will become a
journey that will be your chosen course.
Do not delay, begin today.

276

With every step taken in the direction your
soul speaks, you will feel empowered to take
the next. Transitions can be challenging,
but not so challenging as spending the
duration of your life not doing what
you came here to do.

~

277

Listen to your soul.
It is showing you the way.

278

Messages come in many forms. You co-create them with the All in order to stay on course.

~

279

There are certain things one must ignore in this life. Be sure not to ignore oneself.

280

Be open always to that which resonates on a
soul level. Become increasingly aware
by being so.

~

281

Be kind to others always. There is never an
appropriate time to hurt someone for the sake
of hurting them.

282

'Death' comes to us all,
and yet all are immortal.

~

283

Do not despair if a dear one passes,
for they have not truly left this space. We share
all space, and all are one, you shall always be
connected to them and you shall always be
with them. You may choose to take as many
journeys together as you each wish.

284

Do not be afraid of not getting what you
want in life. You will receive precisely as you
choose. Practice awareness of that which you
are creating and always wish for
the wellness of the All.

~

285

All you ever truly need to know is what step
to take in any moment you feel to. Simply be
present in order to know what this is.

286

Presence is a great gift. It is all that is.
You may experience the All in real time at
any given moment.

~

287

All there is, is available in every moment.
To access this vast wisdom simply be present
and do as thy feel.

288

'Letting go' plays an enormous part in
being able to be here now.

~

289

Do not be afraid of being present.
You hold all the powers of the Universe,
and you deserve to do so. We are all one.
In wisdom of this you hold the
wisdom of the All.

290

There is truly nothing to fear. All that
is happens precisely as it must in order for
expansion to occur and for us to all essentially
flourish. Take on each experience with valor
and commitment. Presence is power.

~

291

You are each changing the world with every
thought, feeling and action. Are you aware of
what it is you are contributing and why? Does
this feel right on a soul level? What might you
wish to do, think or feel differently?

292

Is there something you have been avoiding?
Begin here in finding your way to a
path of presence.

~

293

Presence is all in unison. Humans must
practice their awareness for they are not
separate but believe themselves to
be in almost all cases.

294

When one is present one holds the key
and the lock to all that is.

~

295

Presence is purity of oneness.

296

Once all are conscious of their oneness
with all else, there will be a great merging,
and we will expand at a rate
never found before.

~

297

There will always be all that is. Do not fear
the end, for all is always all. Nothing ever truly
separates, and nothing ever truly comes
to an end. All is always one.

298

When you were a child you had visions
of what was possible. 'Memories' from the
other worlds. What were these? Remember
who you are. You are not only the being you
currently identify as. You have been many
men, many beings; and you are now,
and always have been, all that is.

~

299

Listening to oneself is the only way to
do what you came here to do. Take your
imagined time to do this often.
In fact, always.

300

Become that which you already are.

~

301

Listen to thyself and in turn 'become' the All.

302

You are all already the All; once conscious of this intrinsic truth, all will shift exponentially. Support each other on your journeys.

~

303

Challenge yourself each day to do that which you have resisted out of fear. Decipher what it is that you wish to do upon a soul level. It is not always comfortable but will always lead to greater comfort for the All.

304

Being with yourself is as important as being
with others. Be sure to find balance within
the All and you will bring balance
to the All.

~

305

By simply listening to yourself you
will most affectively be able to achieve what
you came to this planet to do.

306

Notice the clouds, they speak to you.

~

307

Treat others with kindness and this
will be reflected back unto you. This is a
simple energetic law for all affects all in
a reflective manner.

308

If you seek happiness, gift it unto others.

~

309

If you wish for love, find the ways available to
you by which you may love others.

310

If you seek wisdom, listen to thyself and
follow your intuitive guidance to take the
steps available to you in continuation
of your journey.

~

311

By listening to oneself,
one is able to hear the All.

312

By simply deciding to do as you feel in
each moment you are changing the world.

~

313

Actively do as thy feel, always.
You are each as a puzzle piece and the
world can only be in perfect harmony when
each of you plays your part, as insignificant
as that part may seem.

314

It is best for you and all others that
you do as you feel.

~

315

Making decisions must always be from
a place of purity of both mind and heart.
Be sure to still your mind and listen to your
heart. These in unison will always show you
the way. Paths can be complex but with the
guidance available to you, you will have all
you need upon your path.

316

Are there things you are doing in your life
that that you do not need or feel to do?
If this feels to be the case, it is time for
a cleansing of sorts. The time and energy
spent on such endorsements may be spent
instead doing that which you wish and
in turn helping you to solve the 'problems'
that you face. Create harmony with the tools
that you have. Do not be afraid to disappoint
others for doing what is best for you on a
soul level is what is best for all others.

~

317

Gifting kindness unto others is like buying
yourself a gift. Do it as often as you feel.

318

Friends are like gems in a necklace. You are
all a part of the same circle and look most
beautiful when you shine together.

~

319

Visualize what it is that your soul wishes for.
Focus only upon this.
It will bring it into being.

320

There is no need to create anything in this world other than what you feel to upon a soul level. Always listen to oneself. Your energies expand when doing as you deeply feel.

~

321

Be kind to everyone for no one is truly a 'stranger.'

322

Take the time each day to simply 'be.'
This way you may be with the All.

~

323

By listening to oneself, one is able to access
the All and to affect it most profoundly.

324

Everything is all that is. Any one thing and
all the things. We are all the All. Comprehend
this and you will be all powerful.

~

325

Breath is an instant way to consciously
'collect' all that is within oneself.

326

You, by doing that which you came here to do, will be the change you wish to occur upon this world. As seemingly insignificant as this may seem, it truly is the most powerful play you can make.

~

327

Search not outside of you for that which lies within.

328

The Earth, its crust, everything within it and
everything 'outside' of it are all one being.
You are that being. And so am I.

~

329

Trees are gateways between the Earth and the
'heavens' for they understand that they are
the All. Confer with them, they hold
all the wisdom that is.

330

Treat your 'pets' as you would wish to be
treated, for all beings are as sacred
as one another.

~

331

Listening to the All is as simple as simply
being. Being is not inactive. Being is taking
place within the play of all things
as it occurs.

332

'Transcendence' is simple. It is understanding
your oneness with all that is.

~

333

You are much like water,
transforming constantly. If you choose,
you may be consciously at one with the All,
and in so being attain all that is
available to you.

334

There really is nothing but oneness;
and since we are all one, we may do all that
we wish to do. Awareness of what you desire
upon a soul level is all that is truly required.

~

335

Be all that you are, that is all that is.

336

By simply taking the time each day to do
that which you desire upon a soul level, one
opens portals of understanding and possibility;
shifting all in existence so that all may be
as one desires upon a soul level.

~

337

All that is, is the way that it is because of you
all and those 'before' you. The possibilities of
life are infinite by nature. By doing as you feel
upon a soul level you may stretch the bounds
of your previous conception and change all
that is for yourself and the All.

338

Trees are beings just as important and as sophisticated as yourselves. Treat them with due respect and remember that they are (as you have the ability to be) portals / receptors to the All. You may, with their permission, access the All by simply being in their presence. Treat all with kindness and respect, always. Nothing belongs to you and yet you are all that is.

~

339

Your powers are infinite. In order to experience your optimum ability, know thy oneness with the All.

340

Surround the globe with your
mind and know that it is within you. Now
surround the Universe with your mind and
know that you are at one with all things, as is
the territory upon which you walk.
Nothing is not you.

~

341

Oneness simply means home. We are always
home, no matter how far we may feel we have
strayed. There is nowhere that is not this place.
We are always one, everywhere.

342

Good is representative of purity.
Yet no thing can be pure without
process. Enjoy to bask in its rays, but do
not avoid the toil and the trails that you have
yet to endure. You are here for many reasons,
living amidst a vast dimension of web like
fractals, shifting with every breath of the All.
By doing as you feel within this world, you
will affect all others and by being present to
this process one is able to co-create
purity within the All.

~

343

Simply be. This is not lazy. One may be amidst
great action or endurance. This is advanced,
though you are all most capable of such.

344

Dreaming is most important.
Do not forget to dream.

~

345

Presence is a portal to awareness/ all that is.
Be there somewhere more important to be?

346

This suit of flesh and bones that you
wear is not infinite, treat it with the utmost
care and respect. It can take you to the places
you came here to be, and the way by which
you treat your body is the way by which you
are treating your current world.

~

347

Do as you feel; perhaps to paint, to sing,
laugh, love. Do not do as you are told by
others unless it feels upon a soul level to be
what is right for you in any moment. You will
find as you do as you feel in each moment
that synchronicities are most able to take place
and the All is forming with greater purpose.

348

If your life is not functioning as you will it to
be, then look closely at that which you may
be avoiding. As irrelevant as this may seem,
it is likely to be the very key to your success.
Now remember, 'success' in these terms speaks
of that which you came here to do, or that
which you wish to do upon a soul level and
not necessarily that which you consciously
think is best for you.

~

349

Spend periods of time in nature as
often as life permits and as often as you feel to.
This will help you to understand your oneness
with all that is. It is never separate from you
and speaks to you in a thousand languages.

350

Use your breath. Listen to the All.

~

351

Clouds are beautifully representative of all that is. Observe their journey. Watch their transformations. We are all like the cloud.

352

We are all, without true division, all that is.
When one can comprehend this, one will feel
the capacity of the All. It is infinite
and ever expanding.

~

353

If you think you have no time to simply be,
or to listen to yourself and to do the things
you feel to do, then indeed you will not for
you are forming all that is with your thoughts
in every moment. Do as thy feel, I assure you
it is a much more worthwhile use of your
boundless creative abilities.

354

Color is a wonderful tool to use for your healing. It surrounds each of you. 'Tune in' to that which resonates/that which you need by simply seeing what you feel. We are all absorbing color all the time. Choose carefully that which you wish to be 'surrounded' by.

~

355

Humans are a complex species; each are different and yet all are one. Be patient, kind and compassionate with one another. You are a symbol of peace, and as you learn to get along with one another, so too does the All come into harmony. Thank you.

356

Identify that which you have been a
voiding and shift your priorities to
accommodate that which you feel.

~

357

You chose your family; this may be a clear
blessing or may feel like an absolute mistake.
When you chose them, you knew precisely
what you were doing. Honor these wishes.
You have much to learn and much to gain as
well as much to give. Listen always to yourself,
upon a soul level. Do always as you feel.

358

Do not simply tell your child what to do.
Help them to understand what it is that
they feel and why you make the choices that
you make so that they may make their own
without the confines of conditioning.

~

359

Forgive those whom do not understand thee,
else you are dealing the same unto them.

360

Compassion is a great gift, and it is ever available to all to use in abundance.

~

361

To be in grace is to be in presence and to step in harmony with the All.

362

Is there a way by which you wish to change your life? Is there truly a reason not to? Is there a step in this direction available to you now? If not seemingly so, is there something you feel to do but have been avoiding or not noting? Begin here, now.

~

363

What are you consuming, in the form of food, news, literature, film etc.? Is this what you wish to be surrounded by? Might this need editing or adding to? Listen to thyself.

364

Is there something you have been avoiding?
Begin here in finding your way to a
path of presence.

~

365

The creatures upon this planet have much to
teach you. Listen to their words, they speak
in sounds but they are just as sophisticated
as you are. Some day you will cease to need
language at all, indeed it is not a sign of true
sophistication, only a pathway to it.

366

Language can be such a bore. Life is so
entirely limitless. Think beyond thought.

~

367

Do not be shackled by the imaginings
of intellectualism. Wisdom is power, not
apparent knowledge. Use your mind as a tool
and your heart as a guide. Both are powerful
and neither work well without
each other in unison.

368

You don't have to do anything you don't feel
to upon a soul level.

~

369

Are you eating, doing or saying
something you don't feel to? Is there
something else you would like to eat, do or
say instead? Changing your life and the world
in turn is so very simple. Do as thy feel.
All changes, all the time.

370

Discipline means doing as thy feel.
Do not allow yourself to be 'disciplined' by
others. You may take guidance and inspiration
as long as it resonates upon a soul level. To do
as you feel is the easiest approach to existing
upon this, or indeed any other realm.
It is existence within harmony.
It is a pathway of 'light.'

~

371

Children have much to teach us.
Be sure to listen.

372

Presence is man's greatest gift,
for it is the gift of all things at once.

~

373

By listening to your soul's speaking,
you are listening to the soul of the world.
The soul of the world is the soul of the All.

374

Surround yourself by that which
resonates. Do not invest in anything that
does not feel correct on a soul level, no matter
the apparent benefits. Those whom have the
courage and abundance to do as they feel
will be granted with awareness of the All.
There is nothing greater.

~

375

If your life is functioning with great
prosperity, look with awareness at how you
may help the All to flourish in extension of
yourself. You will feel the benefits of this also,
for you are all things and you are all people.

376

If you need help, do not be afraid to ask
for it of those who surround you. If you
are not however taking the steps available to
you then do not expect your circumstances to
alter greatly. We each create patterns, puzzles
to learn from and will continue in doing
so until our lessons have been learned or
our gifts have been given.

~

377

Give away anything that you feel to,
no thing truly belongs to anyone anyway.
Listen always to yourself upon a
soul level and do as you feel.

378

Kindness results in greater world awareness,
for all are one.

~

379

Protect creatures who have not the
ability to protect themselves. This world is
in a state of apparent imbalance and to bring
things into balance, we must help one
another as I am helping you now
from the and apparent above.

380

'Love' one another, for you are all one.
Each and every one of you.

~

381

Your greatest power is that you are all things.
All people, all beings, all one.

382

Listening to oneself is listening to the All.
Simply hear what one speaks upon
a soul level.

~

383

By simply being, one is able to behold
their resonance with the All and to be at
their optimum in being a contributor to the
All. We are all the All, all the time. By taking
the time to just be, one is able to know this
and to become one with all that
is on a conscious level.

384

Your brains are nothing but cells of the All,
indeed you beings are but cells of the All.
You are all, all of the All.

~

385

Building blocks of time contribute
to all else that is, however time does
not exist and the bricks with which you
imagine your reality are nothing but the
imaginings of you and those before you
and these too can be reconstructed.
All is available to you all.

386

Since we are in a state of merging, all that has
ever been possible in any one realm is now
available to you here. Choose intuitively
my dear ones. All is at stake.

~

387

Since you are at one with all beings,
essentially one being, you may witness or
experience the existence of all other beings
that you come into contact with (or indeed
those you do not). Become one with the All
and know the fullness of your truth.

388

You are one with all that is, be it seemingly 'good' or 'bad.' Remember this when you condemn or congratulate another.

~

389

By being the unique vessel of the All that you are, you will form into the most perfectly fitting puzzle piece for all that is to slot together with/ harmonize with/ combine with.

390

It is important to be present when others
speak, and to truly listen. That way you may
note what speaks to the soul, so that you may
become two souls that are speaking, and not
diluted replications of your true selves.

~

391

Do not assume you know better than
another, or that you know best. There is
much to learn from every soul you come into
contact with and many ways by which to
learn from them. You have crossed
paths by your own creation.

392

Love, respect and gratitude are all gifts that
one receives by giving. Be generous with your
distribution of these riches.

~

393

Do not blame others for your life's lessons,
for you chose each of them. Instead, ask
oneself why you gifted yourself with
such opportunities and what have
you to learn from each.

394

By doing as you feel you may avoid much redirection by your All, the greater 'you,' assisting you to re-find your path.

~

395

Love all for you are all the All.

396

Oneness is all that is.

~

397

As you each expand, so too does the Universe.

398

Listening is key to understanding.

~

399

By taking the time for yourself and others you
may honor all that is, by extension
of yourself for we are all one.

400

Allow the path of a bird to remind you
of your direction and you will not falter.
All is displayed in all ways. Pay attention
to its forces, the force by which
you were forged.

~

401

You are much like the wind, the clouds, the
rain. Transforming constantly. Transformation
the only constant. Be here now, and be the
most powerful version of yourself
for nothing else truly exists.

402

Like leaves from a tree, you may shed your
previous conditioning and change as you feel
to in this great world. Do not let anything, or
anyone stop you from doing that which you
feel. Renew yourself with each breath.
You are the All.

~

403

Guidance from others, though true
for them, may be untrue or irrelevant
to you. Be aware of what resonates upon
a soul level and follow only this. Others
may guide you to finding this,
though each person's path
is their own.

404

Allow the sun to flow unto you like a river of
gold. You have now, and will always have all
that you need in this world to receive
the lessons you came here for.

~

405

By taking the time to do as one feels
in every moment, one may be at one with
the All at all times; 'heightening' the vibration
upon this realm, and inter-affecting
all others in union.

406

If you wish to 'change the world,'
simply identify what it is you feel to do in
every moment. This may be a most simple act.
Do not doubt your power, it is immense.

~

407

Listen to the wind, it speaks to you all of that
which is real, is now, is All.

408

Breathe and delight in all that is.

~

409

Breath is key to oneness consciousness.

410

Allow the All to flow through you with
trust and gratitude.

~

411

Once there was just one, now there are
apparently many. We will always be that
which we were, that which we are. No
matter how many multiples are in process;
we are now and shall always be one. So no
one is truly alone, no one is truly separate
and in a sense, it is still the case that the
whole is all that exists. Nothing can exist
outside of us, no one can be separate.

All are one, always.

412

When you honor the All, you honor yourself.
When you honor yourself, you honor the All.

~

413

Contentment only comes from helping
yourself and others, for all are one.

414

All will be 'happy' when all are aware of their
oneness. This is intrinsic to you and yet you
have been taught that separation is truth.
In truth, nothing is separate.

~

415

Specify what it is you wish to create
in the world, not with your mind but
by tapping into all that is. By doing what
you feel to on a soul level. This is how
one creates at their optimum.

416

You design your reality by frequency.
What is it you are emitting?

~

417

Take pleasure in creating and create only that
which you wish upon a soul level.
It is what you are here to do.

418

You are all creators, design within grace.

~

419

There is consistently available to you all the
wonders of not only this world but all others.
You are the All. Behold the All.

420

Calm your mind so that your soul may speak.

~

421

Listen to your soul, it speaks great wisdoms
but much like a person who is wise but will
not fight to express themselves, you will only
be able to hear your true self if you quieten
the person you believe yourself to be.
You are the All.

422

You are an energetic structure
(currently and indeed always). In this
particular structure you will find it most
useful to connect one's current with that of
the All. Choose what resonates upon a soul
level and absorb all that you need from
that which apparently surrounds you.

~

423

Learn about the energetic centers
within oneself. You, as an apparent whole,
are indeed an energetic center/structure and
it will be most useful to you to understand
how this works. You are an expression of the
All through energetic force or 'light.'
Do with this what thy will.

424

Deep 'resonance' is the beginnings of 'physical' oneness. You have the ability to transform in every moment. Do so in direction of oneness.

~

425

Eat only what feels correct, your body will speak to you of these truths,
listen.

426

Ignoring oneself creates 'chaos' to catapult one
back onto their perfect path.

~

427

We are each existent within, and as part of,
perfect patterns. By listening to oneself, one
is able to perform at one's optimum, as a
part of the harmonious whole.

428

Color is vibrancy.
You are all color.

~

429

'Light' is all that is, or 'energy' is all that is.
Do not imagine otherwise for it is truly
quite simple. We are all 'light' or 'energy,'
and we are all one.

430

Much complexity leads to much simplicity.
We have separated only to return to oneness
upon a conscious and complete level. There is
not an end to this journey, however there will
be 'resolve.' Oneness consciousness leads to
greater expansion and greater possibility.

~

431

Listen to the creatures that surround you,
for you are a part of nature and what the
All says is very much relevant to you.

432

Do not assume that you are 'more evolved' than any other being because of your ability to control. This is an illusion.

~

433

There are many gifts upon this planet in the form of medicinals. One need not look further than the nature that surrounds one to heal all ailments upon this plane.

434

Build what you wish with your
tools of creation, for you are creating
with every breath, every step,
every thought, every feeling.

~

435

Listen to your soul,
it holds the answers that you seek.

436

Do not disdain that which you do
not understand, instead seek to weigh it
by resonance with your soul and decide
from there what is necessary to absorb.
Much of that which is taught is misleading.
The truth is that all changes all the time, by
co-creation. Always fact check the truth with
one's soul's resonance and alter by
creation that which you feel.

~

437

Co-creation is how the
Universe is continuing to form.

438

Minds are useful for pondering ideas but be
sure not to allow them to make the decisions.

~

439

Growth is happening in every moment.
Choose carefully in which direction you grow,
towards the light is most affective.

440

Drink plenty of water for it is a part of
you and you are a part of it. It is a necessary
element of life upon this plane and one from
which each of the cells that build your
body may benefit greatly. Do not
underestimate its powers,
nor your own.

~

441

By listening to oneself,
one will know all that is.

442

Do not ignore oneself.
Define what it is you have been ignoring and
actively work to do the opposite. Zone in on
the specific thing(s) that need(s) to be done,
accepted, pondered upon and do so with
grace and courage. There is nothing to fear
and the easiest way to navigate one's
path is by listening to oneself.

~

443

Listen carefully to your soul's speakings,
they will describe to you in great detail that
which is harmonious, that which is graceful,
that which is in step with the All.

444

Sick of this job/ town/ situation? Ask oneself:

1. Why might I have designed it this way?
2. What steps are available to me
to change direction?
3. Who am I and why did I come here?
(If you're not sure, learn to be quiet and listen
to oneself. You can only discover this from
self, not from asking others.)

~

445

Be as kind to oneself as you wish others to be
to you. You are not separate, and
all reflects the All.

446

All is available to you all the time.

~

447

There is no rush to return to that which
you already are.

448

Numbers are nothing but everything that is,
everything that is, is nothing but numbers.

~

449

With each step in harmony with the All,
one co-forms the entirety of all that is
in perfect harmony.

450

There is nothing upon this plane,
nor any other, that you are not.

~

451

Do not purchase anything that you do not
resonate with. Promote only the existence
of that which you do.

452

If you are sick, ask yourself why it is that
you have asked for this upon a soul level.
This may sound 'harsh' but indeed is the way
of things, for in this life, or before you even
entered life upon this realm, a suggestion
or decision was made by you for great
reason. You are not a 'victim' of this,
you are a receiver of its teachings.
What chose you to learn?

~

453

Pay great attention to 'visions.' Indeed this
'life' itself is a sort of vision, and they come in
many forms, all of which to teach us
that which we wish to learn.

454

Do not be disheartened by those whom distrust or disbelieve you, for you chose them to commune with in order to learn. Whence one is able to be themselves in their entirety, despite the energy of 'others,' one is able most powerfully to benefit the All.

~

455

Color is most important. Surround yourself only by that which you feel, for all affects the All. A mere decoration detail may be having an immense effect on your 'psyche.' Your mind represents your body in frequency (and your body represents your mind in frequency) and each represent the All.

456

Distill and settle your thoughts,
this will in turn settle that which
apparently surrounds you.

~

457

Listen to the trees, they know
much more than
can be told.

458

Breathe in the light, for it surrounds and
bathes you, even in apparent darkness.

~

459

You are light; and with each breath of this
eternal resource you make yourself,
and the whole, greater still.

460

Do not, not do something because it
seems 'obvious.' Indeed, do that which
seems obvious to you and which feels
correct in unison. Sometimes the most
effective ways of changing the world are
in plain sight. Always do that which is best
for you and in turn the All, or best for the
All and in turn for you. There is nothing that
benefits only you, the above are consistently
synonymous. Do not be taken by illusions
of disguise. Do always what <u>feels</u> correct
upon a soul level.

~

461

You may breathe in the 'sun' through your
energetic centers. This will empower you
to do what it is you came here to do.

462

I will assist you with what it is you came
here to do. Be quiet. Breathe. Listen.

~

463

When your journey here is over,
do not despair; rejoice in the knowing that
you have completed a great journey, and that
you begin another. That you have option to
continue to co-create all that is with whom
you wish and that you will never be separate
from your loved ones, though no more in
this particular form. What a great number of
forms you have yet to enjoy, and which you
used to identify as. All is ever existing.

464

Do not be afraid to run out of time, for time does not exist and you are each eternal.

~

465

Do not fear separation with others at the apparent end of your life, for in 'death' one is reminded of the union of all things, of the truth that you are never truly separate.

466

Do as you feel; this may include doing very little at times, at others it may be great action. Find balance within oneself and one will reflect it into the All and this will be self-perpetuating.

~

467

If your life is in turmoil ask yourself what step you have available to you to walk in grace, in harmony with the All. Though times may be tumultuous you are on track to finding a greater sense of balance. This may be found only by taking the steps available to you that resonate upon a soul level. There are always steps available to one. Breathe in and know what feels correct.

468

Do not disdain your chosen realm.
Instead, use your presence to change that
which you wish to be different.

~

469

By listening to your heart, you may hear
the resonance of the All.

470

God is All.
You are God. Nothing is not God.

~

471

We are each creators.
Mistake not that there is only one creator,
though we are all one.

472

The very most 'sensible' thing to do
is precisely as one feels.

~

473

Decide now to be present, and from this day
forth commit to doing that which you feel
upon a soul level. What a perfect stance
from which to do that which
you came here to do.

474

Nourish not only yourself but that
which apparently surrounds you, for it is a
part of you/you are a part of the All.

~

475

Take care of all in your apparent
possession. Even if you purchased it, it is
a gift worth honoring and indeed nothing
stays with you unless it is carefully cared for.
This, as many things do, applies beyond this
realm, this life. Be 'loving' to all, in gratitude/
appreciation of all. This takes time which
in turn you create as you wish it to be.

476

Since you create time, you may create it as you wish it to be. Fill it with that which you feel upon a soul level, and all will alter to accommodate your wishes.

~

477

Everything is 'growing,' altering, shifting, morphing. Do not expect otherwise and literally go with the flow which you co-create.

478

'Going with the flow' does not mean to sit back and let the All sweep you up and do as it wills with you: it means acknowledging that you are a unique and powerful part of the All and that by doing exactly as you feel you may collaborate most affectively.

~

479

Allow yourself time to simply 'be.' It is an important aspect of successful living.

480

One cannot achieve all they came here to do
without honoring themselves.

~

481

Take care of your health. If you prioritize this,
then so too will the All.

482

Co-form your reality as you wish it to be.

~

483

By simply doing as you feel, you create
your reality as you wish to be.

484

Take the time always to do as you feel,
else you are creating that which
you do not wish for.

~

485

There are many things one must do that one
wishes not to but feels to upon a soul level. Be
astutely aware of the difference. Do always as
you feel to upon a soul level.

486

No one has ever truly flourished without
helping others upon their journeys.

~

487

No man may be truly happy in life without
bringing happiness unto others.

488

By listening to oneself one may hear
the resonance of the All and detect its unique
place and play within it.

~

489

Be of comfort to others and one will find
their own path is made smooth.

490

Love generously. Love is ever expansive.

~

491

You are an architect of reality.
What is it that you are building, moment
by moment, thought by thought?

492

You are creating, right now and always.
What are you choosing?
What is it that you truly believe?
Then it shall be.

~

493

Gratitude is one of the greatest
gifts from which everyone receives,
and through which all expands.

494

Care for your plants, your creatures and
your home as you wish to be cared for
upon this plane. They are all in a sense
an extension of you, and you cannot
fully flourish without also nurturing
them to the best of your ability,
for all reflects the All.

~

495

Plants are representative of force in form.
How might you express the All in
your apparent physicality?

496

Create only that which you wish to upon a soul level and curate energetic structure in collaboration with harmony.

~

497

If you wish to change the world, simply do as you feel. You change it with every thought, every breath, every moment.
All is change, always.

498

Detangle and edit your possessions, most of
you have far too many things. Care for that
which you intuitively choose to keep.
Go by feeling, not only thought.

~

499

Listen to that which your home says to you,
if a draw or a closet is quietly demanding
to be organized then oblige its calls, it is
reflective of all else in your reality.

500

One may begin to powerfully create
harmony in one's world by simply cleaning
out a closet or sweeping a floor.

~

501

One will find that as they honor their
intuitions their world comes into harmonic
alignment and miracles ensue. Alignments
come into place that could not have without
your taking the steps available to you. Allow
this to encourage you to continue upon
your chosen path.

502

When existing from a place of presence and gratitude one feels all that is and so becomes consciously all that is. From this place only, one may be all powerful.

~

503

Listen to your soul. It speaks the truth, for each of you know all truths upon a soul level. Use this precious resource. It is available to all of you at all times; but only to those whom quiet their minds.

504

Your mind's eye sees all
for you each are the All.

~

505

Bring forth what it is you wish to create,
for you each have a quest and you each know
upon a soul level what that is. You may only
know the first step; you may not know where
it leads. Do always as you feel upon a soul
level and your path will expand with
each step that you take.

506

By simply being, one may feel the All. By
feeling the All, one may behave in response to
all that is in live time. All is shifting constantly;
by responding to all that is from a place of
presence, one may be empowered by reality as
it is in each moment, rather than responding
to a reality which has already altered.
Presence is power.

~

507

By gifting unto others the gifts that
have been bestowed upon you, one may be
free of the illusion of separation, for all are
one and one may only fully flourish in the
love and assistance of others.

508

You each have a 'quest' or a 'mission,'
or many in fact. Do as you feel and your
work upon this realm may be successfully
completed. Do not be distracted by earthly
successes, these may be included in your
quests or may deter from them.
Simply do as you feel.

~

509

You each hold all the
wisdoms of the Universe.
What remarkable beings you are.

510

You are all powerful when you know
your oneness with the All.

~

511

Riches are not meant for hoarding.
All is meant for sharing,
for you are all the All.

512

Forgiveness is one of the greatest gifts you can
give to yourself and others.

~

513

Be as the tree, with limb and leaf
stretched toward the light and your roots
firmly grounded unto the earth.

514

Respect your planet for it is a part of you.

~

515

Love and respect all beings,
despite your differences. It is the quest of
humans at large to become in harmony with
one another and as they do, so too will
the multiverse co-form in peace.

516

Do not be disheartened by others lack
of understanding. Instead, focus upon the
teachings available to you and in turn
the expansion of the All.

~

517

Take joy and peace from that which
surrounds you, where it cannot be found
grant that unto the world.

518

Listen to those whom have messages to
share with you; never assume you already
know what it is that others have to share with
you. Use your heart as a filter for truth
and act only on that which resonates.

~

519

There is much to learn from everything one
experiences. The very most sophisticated
thing to understand is your
oneness with all that is.

520

Each challenge is a blessing and a lesson.
Ask yourself "why might I have 'chosen'
or 'co-created' this?"

~

521

Lessons come in many forms and answers
come sometimes in an unusual order. Become
acutely aware of that which you are receiving,
your gifts are in constant inflow.

522

That which you are wishing for is that which
you are receiving. Instead of asking 'why is
this happening to me?' try asking 'why am I
choosing this? Why am I creating this?
What have I to learn from this?'

~

523

By living this life in the present moment,
one may achieve what they came here to do.
You are not the person you are expressing in
this current lifetime. You are the All expressing
itself in individual form. Your life is extremely
important. Be sure to do as you feel, in unison
with the All. It is the only way to achieve
all that you came here to do.

524

By simply being, one is able to respond
to/ work with the All as all happens;
this is the very most effective way of
'living.'

~

525

Since we are all essentially one 'being,' by
doing as one feels one is responding to the
All and doing as one feels/ as is appropriate
as a whole. This may not conform to what
seems appropriate culturally. By doing as
you feel upon a soul level one assists in
creating the All at its fullest potential, on
its journey toward greater expansion
and harmony in oneness.

526

By listening to oneself, one may hear the All.

~

527

Bypass your mind as needed. Be nimble.
Tune in to your heart as you might
an instrument in an orchestra.
Tune in to the All.
You are all a part of it.

528

You cannot fully flourish unless
that which surrounds you flourishes, that
which surrounds you cannot fully flourish
unless you do also, as you are all one.

~

529

Seek to nourish yourself and others as
you are all essentially one.

530

What is the very best solution, for you and all
others at any time, seek to find this, without
compromise. Transform darkness into light,
bring balance forth where chaos ensues.

~

531

Be a creator at your most powerful,
do all that you do for the All.

532

Nurture your mind so that it may rest, that way you will hear your heart and navigate with greater consciousness.

~

533

Listen to the wind, it speaks to you clearly of all that is. Watch the plants, the trees, and the dust as they describe these teachings through form.

534

You already know all that is.

~

535

Do not despair in being upon
the plane of your own choosing. Instead
do what it is you came here to do. Escaping
this reality will likely result in your return
to it. Be present upon this plane, you chose to
be here, no doubt for a good reason as
you held perspective of all that is.

536

Doing as you feel is the very most
direct route to achieving all you came here to
do. Have you something more important to
do than that?

~

537

Listen to yourself, be patient with yourself,
be kind to yourself.
You are the All.

538

You are each all that is, you are wonderful,
we are wonderful. We are all one, my brethren.

~

539

By listening to oneself one may experience
oneness.

540

In order to honor the All one must
honor themselves and that which they feel.
Do not be self-sacrificial unless you feel to
be upon a soul level. That which serves you,
serves the All. Navigate with grace. Do
always as you feel upon a soul level,
in harmony with the All.

~

541

Much change is afoot upon this plane; in
order to stay afloat simply ride the waves we
have co-created and create new ones formed
of harmony. You may truly create that which
you wish to upon a soul level.

542

Do not be afraid of chaos, it is guiding
you to the light of which you are made.

~

543

All reflects the All, all affects the All.

544

Chaos and harmony are brother and sister.
Listen to the lessons of each, do as you can
always to bring all into harmonic balance.
This is your gift and your quest.

~

545

Humans are instigators of harmonic balance.
They are free to take whatever path they wish;
all paths lead to balance and time
does not exist.

546

Do not doubt your greatness
for you are all that is.

~

547

Kindness is self-care for you are all one.

548

Be as kind to yourself as you are to others,
for you are all one. Be as kind to others as
you are to yourself, for you are all one.

~

549

Remove the obstacles you display to
yourself. You must have put them there for
a reason. What have I to learn from this?
Why might I have designed my reality
this way? What next step(s) feel most in
flow with the All/ expansion?

550

Listen to the trees, they speak between realms.

~

551

Listen to, love and commune with
your Earth, for you are a part of it and it is
a part of you, most directly. The surface of
the Earth is akin to your own skin. It wishes
for acknowledgement as you do. You are
together always upon this plane.
Be friends. Be one.

552

By listening to yourself you can hear all that is
in real time. Since all is changing all the time,
this is the most powerful place to be.

~

553

We co-create all that is.
What do you wish to contribute to the All?

554

Listen to your soul.
It speaks quietly of all that is.

~

555

Breathe.
Not only into your nostrils but every cell.
Vitality comes in many forms.

556

Generosity is the best way of receiving
that which you wish for. Sharing with the
All in the wisdom that we are all one.

~

557

Be kind to yourself and others.
Each of you are imperative to the All.
You are all the All.

558

Do not take on others' problems as your own. Intuit ways by which to help others and remain in the balance of the energy you wish to be surrounded by/ a part of.

~

559

Do not doubt your own greatness.
You are each a representation of all that is, in physical form. You are each reflective of the All. You each have the ability to love, to create and to be in awe of the wonders of all that is.

560

Do not be afraid of your own powers.
You were created to assist in the expansion
of the All. Your powers are immense.
You are all that is.

~

561

You are beautiful at your best; you are
beautiful at your 'worst.'
You are the All.

562

Encourage and compliment others
when you feel to. We are all doing our best
and require the support of one another. The
simplest compliment may help someone to
continue upon a courageous path. Each being
upon the planet, and indeed all others, has
a unique quest. All have their challenges. All
beings need the support of the All. Be the
love you wish to exist upon your plane.

~

563

'Manifestation' has been somewhat
misinterpreted. Indeed, you are all 'master
manifestors,' you are each manifesting all of
the time. The key is listening to your soul and
working in unison with the All to contribute
to the co-creation of the All at your/ our
optimum. This is not about creating wealth
for oneself. It is about wholistic expansion
at our greatest potential.

564

Be patient with yourself and others.
You are each doing your best, and that
which is obvious to one may be a blind
spot for another. Be assured that upon this
plane you each have blind spots. Rather
than becoming frustrated by another's,
look more closely for your own.

~

565

Love is the union of all that is, expressing itself
in a multitude of ways. Love deeply,
love purely, love expansively.

566

Forgive others,
it is a gift both to them and to yourself.

~

567

Let kindness and respect be your guide,
your anchor, your goal.
Always.

568

Allow others to develop at their own pace.
Focus upon your own path and acutely note
each step available to you as it forms.

~

569

You have nothing to fear. Fear creates
only what you do not wish for. Focus instead
upon that which you wish for, that which
resonates upon a soul level.

570

What is it you wish to attract into your
existence? Emit this.

~

571

Become aware of the feeling of that
which no longer resonates. That which
requires 'letting go' of. Be in constant change
with the All, be ever upgrading to
that which resonates.

572

Your mind is almost obsolete.
Be sure to use your mind, do not let it
use you. Focus priority on that which you
feel, not that which you think. Thought is
co-formed of that which has been.
Feeling permits expression that is
truly new, original, present.

~

573

Dedicate time each day to yourself.
How can you heal the whole if your
immediate vessel needs care and
is being neglected?

574

If you knew precisely how much time
you had left upon this plane, you would
no doubt use it most consciously. Perhaps
treat each day as if there lies before you a
perfect world just waiting to be painted.
Know in your being what part you
have to play and play it endlessly.

~

575

Know your oneness with all that is.
It is all that is.

576

Welcome that which is new, that which stretches your mind, your reality. Use your soul's guidance to navigate such territories. One may only grow when there is space for the unknown in which to grow.

~

577

Always check in with your feelings. How do I truly feel about this? It will save you a lot of time and useless pondering.

578

Sometimes things need to be
thought through. Most of the time things
need to be felt through. Save time by
jumping to the latter.

~

579

You may ignore yourself as
often as you wish, your experiences
will continue to bring you back on
track, regardless of your deviations for
you are in co-creation of the Universe
and there is no other outcome available
but eventual expansion. To which
degree you contribute to wholistic
expansion is entirely up to you.

580

Deepen your desire to do as you wish.
You have been rewarded for doing as you
have been told for the most part. Now be
aware of the rewards of echoing what you feel
unto the Universe from which your feelings
permeated. There is only reward from doing
that which you feel. Though there may be
rocks in the path, be assured you designed
it that way, no doubt for good reason
for you each know all that is.

~

581

Do not be afraid of anything. You are the
designer of the All. You change anything you
wish. Face fear head on; when it has nowhere
to go it will dissipate. Your strength is beyond
your current comprehension.

582

Listen to thyself.
You know all that is and feel what step
next to take.

~

583

By listening to oneself one is able to detect
harmony as it is co-formed by you.

584

Listen to your intuition, it is awareness of all
that is as if on drip. You each know all there is
to know upon a soul level and have only to be
open to the truth in order to know what it is.

~

585

Each of you is assigned at least one,
if not many, guides. These beings are in
combination both ancestors and/ or light
beings whom assist you upon your journey.
Each are eager to assist you in any way needed
and are ever available to you. You are never
alone; you are always at one with the
All and you always have guides
assisting you on your course.

586

If something feels wrong be sure not to ignore it. Listen to yourself astutely for guidance. You will know what path to take. That which you ignore will only replicate until you face it head on.

~

587

Deal in grace. It is the most sophisticated currency available to you and grows *en masse* as it is expended.

588

Identify that which needs to alter in your existence and any steps available to you in that direction. There are always steps available to each and every one of you, the art is being able to detect them.

~

589

Often the step available to you is ignored for focus upon the goal. One cannot get to the goal in one step and the path is not always obviously mapped. Listen to yourself and take the step that feels integrally correct, even if the correlation is not obvious.

590

We are each tested constantly. Not by
'God,' nor any separate entity but by you
personally; expressed through the All. Each
course is tailor made and co-designed by
you all. Be sure that every detail of your
existence was made that way
for good reason.

~

591

Do not be angered or frustrated by sickness,
instead ask oneself what blessings have come
with such. What lessons are here to be learned.

592

Be kind to others, many behave strangely
because of a lack of love. By loving the All,
you can assist in expedited expansion
and oneness consciousness.

~

593

By assisting others, you are creating a
more sturdy path for oneself.

594

Take the time to speak with children and to
truly listen to them. They carry gifts from
beyond this realm and have much
to teach as well as to learn.

~

595

Be sure to put your hands in the earth from
time to time. You are part of the same being
and grow in force by your union.

596

Switch off from the electronics that you
are accustomed to as often as you may.
You are designed with unfathomable
sophistication and need not cellular
phones to connect across the rays.

~

597

A short walk in nature can
save you a lot of time. Connect to that
which you are one with and know more
accurately what resonates and what does not.
Step with grace and clarity. Accepting that
you know all when you disregard that
you know anything at all.

598

Put your mind to rest and allow your soul
to speak. It holds great wisdom,
all the wisdom of the All.

~

599

Do not hesitate in doing that which you
feel upon a soul level. Train yourself to
prioritize this above all else. This will
always be what is best for others,
as that which is best for you
is best for the All.

600

Do not be concerned what others think of
you, instead focus upon what you feel and
act accordingly. One cannot expect others to
understand one's actions but it is imperative
that we act in accordance with
our integral feelings.

~

601

Choose your company intuitively and spend
plenty of time alone or in the
company of 'animals.'

602

If you wish to change the world,
simply do as you feel.

~

603

Upon the rainbow shines a
full spectrum of color (including colors
currently undetectable to the human eye.)
Absorb that which you feel to by
simply acknowledging and 'tuning into'
the colors that 'surround' you.
Color is medicine.

604

Almost all things have the potential to be medicinal or poisonous. Step carefully, in accordance with your soul's guidance.

~

605

Numbers are an interesting way of describing a realm. All is in a sense numerical but then numbers are just one language with which to describe life. There are many others including light and color. Each represent apparent form. Form is interpretational. All shifts as the All shifts and each apparent form alters as your interpretation of it does.

606

There is nothing that separates
'God' and 'man.' Indeed, we are all 'God.'

~

607

Do not be put off by others' judgements,
focus upon what feels correct/ harmonious
to you. Do not think about it, feel it. You
already know in almost all circumstances, it
is simply a matter of connecting pathways,
reminding oneself of truth resonance.

608

Create harmony in your home and watch it permeate into your existence. The outcome of sorting an unkempt cupboard can be profound beyond words.

~

609

Everything is frequency, including you.

610

You are the light that you seek.

~

611

Disregard thoughts from others which
do not resonate to you, and never take offense
by others misconceptions. You are responsible
for your own thoughts, not that of others.

612

Listen carefully to that which <u>feels</u> correct.

~

613

When others act out of resonance
with the All, there lies an opportunity to
attune oneself with greater precision.

614

Give kindness and respect even
when you do not receive such gifts. A
wise man knows that they are the creator
of the All and that that which you purvey,
you receive overall. Remember we are living
in a multidimensional world in which there is
no beginning nor end. Create light and you
will receive it. Though this may not be
instantaneous, it is the only possible
outcome of your endeavors.

~

615

Being wise means simply to listen.
To yourself. To others. To the All.

616

Prioritize that which you feel to do
upon a soul level. Much time will be saved
by you doing as you came here to do.

~

617

Since one is receiving and emitting
'energy' constantly, choose carefully that
which you receive and that which you emit.
Be sure it is in resonance with your
soul's guidance, and so the All.

618

The climate has always, and will
always, change. The most pressing issue
is the protection of your waters, your air,
and your earth. Poison these and you will
continue to poison yourself. Protect
and care for these, and your own
healthwill reflect such actions.

~

619

The Earth is in extension of you. You are in
extension of the Earth and the All. By caring
for your home as is intuitive to you, you also
protect your own health for all is one.

620

The climate will continue to
change, regardless of your actions.
However, if you choose now to stop polluting
the air, the earth, the waters, then you will
be protecting your own kind.

~

621

Listen to the land upon which
your dwelling sits. It speaks to you.

622

Connect to the fire within you and
within this 'planet.' It is intrinsic to you, not
something to be feared but gently stoked.

~

623

In order to honor oneself and others,
one has simply to listen to one's soul.

624

Do not expect others to do as you would.
They are each unique expressions of the
All and we cannot reach harmonic balance
without them being precisely who they are.

~

625

Be aware of the choices you are making in
life, the work you choose to do, the company
you choose to keep, the way by which you
express yourself in this world. You are a part
its creation and are creating and attracting
that which you are choosing, whether
that be conscious or not.

626

Be very selective of whom you choose to
be intimate with, this is a sacred union. Your
'diseases' are created by lack of consciousness.
Choose consciously these gifts and respect
one another with the awe and admiration
you each deserve.

~

627

Partners may be for a long period or a
seemingly short period. It is important to
realize that each relationship is a gift and is
full of lessons of how to navigate this realm
and the All. Each is an opportunity to love
oneself and others more deeply. Each is a step
in the direction of oneness consciousness
and the merging of the All.

628

Listen to yourself,
and you will hear the All.

~

629

Take care of yourself and you will reflect
such unto the All, look after the All and such
will be reflected unto oneself.

630

Animals, in general, are much wiser than humans. You have much to learn from them. Take the time to do so. Intelligence cannot be measured in thoughts. One who knows all knows there is nothing they do not know.

~

631

Poison and medicine come in the same packaging. Self understands dosage.

632

Put only in your body that which it
wishes to consume.

~

633

When you do precisely as you feel you
allow the All to flow through you.

634

If you are not sure how to spend your 'time'
in this life, simply listen to yourself. To your
soul, to your body. What does it wish for?
Don't do as you think you should,
do as you feel to do.

~

635

Gifts surround each of you. Wealthy is
he whom recognizes these gifts.
They come in many forms.

636

Watching the way by which you conduct
yourself will lend to you living your life the
way you wish to. Almost all of the time it is
oneself whom is in one's way.

~

637

Do not despair if what you wish for
has not yet come to be. Instead, focus more
greatly upon what it is that you wish for and
what it is you have already. The combination
of these energies will assist in co-creating
that which is best for you and the All.

638

Taking the time to simply be each day
is important if you wish to have a peaceful
existence upon this plane.

~

639

Love others.
They are all as sacred as you are,
and you/ we are all 'God.'

640

'God' is a word used to describe the All.
It is not separate from you.
You are all the All.

~

641

Do not be disempowered by the
illusion of separation. Instead, empower
oneself by realizing your true power;
your oneness with all that is.

642

No man can thrive while holding another down. Every action finds its mirror in one form or another. It is important to honor all in existence for you are each all in existence.

~

643

Energy is like light (light in fact is energy) it permeates and reforms yet never disappears.

644

Trust yourself; you know all there is to know
if you are able to bypass your own thought.

~

645

Make choices that resonate on a soul level.
Anything except this will lead to a longer
course in order to provide more
opportunity to do just this.

646

We are all on course.
We are all en route to merge.
We are all one and we will soon be tangibly
so. Though there is 'no time' in your apparent
time, there will be much change in the years
to come. Much death and much rebirth –
upon this realm and others. Do not be afraid
of change. All is always changing. You will
each have profoundly more opportunities as
a result of the changes which are
beginning to occur.

~

647

Do not doubt your ability to do anything
you feel to. You are each a miracle of existence
and can create anything you wish to upon
a soul level.

648

Choose carefully the company you keep.
We are each energetic centers of sorts and it is
important to be fueled by one another and to
make sure that the energy you give out is at
least equal to the energy you absorb. What do
you wish to resonate? What do you wish to
contribute 'energetically?'
Make conscious choices.

~

649

Choosing to be more present upon
this plane is greatly powerful. We each create
most powerfully from a place of presence for
one is in oneness.

650

Love the one you love by allowing them
to be whom they are.

~

651

Beginning in doing that which you
feel on a soul level will result in you feeling
the way you have always wished to feel.
You cannot feel absolute contentment
without listening to yourself and
doing that which you feel to do.

652

You all came to this Earth with purpose. Why are you here? You will remember if you begin in doing as you feel.

~

653

Each soul has many mates. Do not become stuck on the idea of being with one person because they are your 'soul mate.' For some it is appropriate and possible to have many loves. For others it is best for them and the All that they stay with one person. Like all else in existence, do as you feel upon a soul level. Honor yourself and all others and remember that you have much to learn.

654

Friends are nothing but others in
resonance with your own sense of being.
Some will accompany you for a lifetime,
others for many lifetimes. None are
not a part of you.

~

655

When you are alone choose not to distract
yourself. Choose to be present. Choose to be
here. Choose to reconnect with the All.

656

Friends are those whom choose to be in your
company because they truly appreciate who
you are. Be sure to surround yourself with
those whom you appreciate and
who appreciate you.

~

657

Help those in need and be sure
to ask for help when needed.
We are all one my brethren.

658

Find sacred spaces with which you can
resonate and dedicate time to being there.
Reconnect to all that is as often as you can.
You can do so from anywhere, but it is
helpful to connect through nature.

~

659

If you truly love somebody, be sure to support
them in doing what is best for them, even if
that means going another direction.
Love is eternal and need not be
bestowed between two
individuals in order
to exist.

660

Cherish your loved ones and be kind
and respectful to all others. By doing so,
you will create the world at its optimum.
'Heaven' is possible upon this plane.

~

661

Listen to your heart; it asks you to be kind
for it hurts when you are hurtful.

662

Forgiveness is key to contentment.

~

663

When one is in the midst of great turmoil it is often challenging to see the path available. In order to visualize your next steps, simply be still and allow the dust to settle and the air to clear. All may be moving around you, but your own stillness will allow your path to unfold.

664

In this life there are many challenges.
You came to this realm to be a part of the
changes that are taking place here and that are
affecting all else that is. Do not be afraid of
these changes, in choosing to come here you
committed to being a part of such change.
You are each capable of the tasks at hand and
would not have chosen to partake in these
changes otherwise. Have faith in oneself.
Have trust in oneself.

~

665

Listening to one's soul is the best way to
navigate this world. Only you know what is
best for you. Take advice with great care. Only
accept that which resonates with your soul, as
do my words. They are our words. They are
the words of the All.

666

No one is ever truly lost; they are on a
path that will lead them to the destination
intended. All paths lead to the same place;
harmony, balance, and oneness consciousness.

~

667

Always do what is best for you and the All.
If you misstep, carefully re-route. You know
which step is correct in every moment.
Simply quiet your mind and
reconnect to the All.

668

All beings' natural way is to be in balance
with others. We are in process of finding this
balance. We are at a time during which there
will have to be much deconstruction in order
to construct a reality that is in balance. We are
not getting further from this purity of being,
in fact we are nearing it now.

~

669

Be patient with yourself and others. It is
challenging to be upon this realm and the best
way to succeed in that which you came here
to do is to live in support of others.

670

There is so much upon this plane that you do not know, not to mention the eternally expanding continuation of all other realms. Listen to your heart, to your soul, for those are not limited by the imagining that they know, they just do.

~

671

There is great pain upon this plane, sometimes unexplainably difficult to bear. Listen to your soul and know that each experience upon this plane is necessary for the expansion of the All, and that you are not the individual whose part you are now playing, but in fact are all things.

672

Your soul is a fragment of
the soul of the All. You each share in this.
We are all whole as one. You know all
that is for you are all that is.

~

673

If another is unkind to you,
the best way by which to remedy the
situation is to speak from your heart and to
do as feels correct from an 'integral' or soul
level. Bring light to darkness, bring balance to
imbalance. Do not provide likeness of energy
in return, or the unkindness, or imbalance,
will self-perpetuate. Use your gift of
creation to turn darkness into light.

674

Be kind and respectful to all beings.
Have clear boundaries.
Do not be afraid.

~

675

You each have a purpose,
a reason for being. Do you know
consciously what that is? Does that
need further defining? 'Sit' with
yourself and know why it is you are here.
If you cannot figure it out, begin by
acknowledging the small ways in
which you ignore yourself and
begin to listen.

676

What is it that you feel guilty about if anything? What is it that can be done about this? Guilt is a gift; it highlights that which needs to be acknowledged or resolved.

~

677

There is no one upon this plane that is not meant to be here. You each chose to be here.

678

Choose to spend your time doing as you wish
to, for both you and your apparent time are
precious, and your unique energies
are needed upon this plane.

~

679

Virtue is that which you give despite logic.
You are each virtuous on a soul level. Do as
you feel, my brethren, and balance will
be brought forth.

680

We are all whole as one.

~

681

Do not be saddened by others behavior,
instead perfect your own performance of that
which you feel upon a soul level. By doing so
you will change all realms and assist greatly
in bringing us all into harmonic balance.

682

Whatever occurs during your existence, ask oneself 'why might I have chosen this?', 'What have I to learn from this?' Or simply delight in the experience.

~

683

We are all the All. Do not imagine that any element is separate. Do not lend to the illusion of separation.

684

Almost all beings upon this plane are kindred.
Those whom are not, are en route to being so.
Bless all those upon your path and your path
will be laid with jewels.

~

685

The sky transforms as you do.
We are affected by the stars,
and we affect the stars.

686

Do not doubt your power, you are the All.
To access your power in its fullness,
simply be yourself.
You are the All.

~

687

Much 'magic' lays upon this plane. You are
each an example of this. You humans have the
ability to change all that is at a colossal rate.
You may break it, or you may bring all into
balance. We have faith in you and believe
that you will listen to yourselves.

688

Be patient with others, you each learn at
your own pace, and you cannot understand
where another is upon their path for it differs
to yours, though they lead to the same place;
oneness.

~

689

Do not judge others for you cannot
understand where they are coming from.
Instead, with patience and compassion look at
your own behaviors and ask yourself if there
are ways by which you might alter them.

690

Listen to your soul: it is so very simple to
do what you came unto this plane to do.
Simply do as you feel. Each day.
Each moment. Always.

~

691

Be kind always. Protect yourself from harm
but do not respond with harm.

692

Do not curse others nor the Above for your
challenges. You chose them. Why?

~

693

Be kind to yourself. Many are kind to others
but treat themselves unkindly. Be a friend to
yourself, for you are as sacred and
as special as all others.

694

You need not know the fullness of your quest.
Ever available to you is your next step.

~

695

Treat all beings with respect,
this includes the plants in your life for they
too are beings. You cannot flourish fully while
neglecting another in your care.

696

Jealously is something to pay
attention to. Since we are all one,
we benefit fromcelebrating one another's
victories and successes. What is it you wish to
change about yourself, your life? Comparison
is rarely useful, and listening to oneself will
always result in profound steps forward.
You have the power to change your life
and to make it as you wish it to
be upon a soul level.

~

697

Knowing that you are at one with the All
helps one to know that they are 'home' always.
No matter who you are with, no matter
where you are.

698

One needs nothing except the awareness that
they are all things. One has time
to accomplish this.

~

699

Listening to oneself will result in your
conscious understanding of oneness
with all things.

700

Simply do as you feel.
This is in some cases challenging
but always the easiest path.

~

701

Love all beings for you are all beings.

702

Listen to thyself. Thy ist the All.

~

703

By taking the time to feel into what is correct
one saves much time indeed.

704

Do not use your precious time to do that
which you do not wish to do upon this
world. You may have a job that is necessary
for you to achieve that which you came here
to do, which in itself you do not adore, but
if you feel to continue on the path of doing
this job, then do so. If, however, you feel to
move on from this job, then no doubt another
opportunity will arise. Upon a soul level, you
each know which step to take, and when.
Ignoring oneself results in further turmoil.
Listen to oneself, and do as thy
feel on a soul level.

~

705

Religions all stem from the same place.
The seeking of the oversoul. You are each the
oversoul. You have already found 'God' for
you are all that is.

706

You each have the ability to transcend all that
is and to consciously be all that is.
This is a returning to self.

~

707

Do not judge others for their inadequacies.
Each have lessons to learn.

708

You are not separate from nature,
you are nature.

~

709

If you feel 'down,' ask oneself:
What can I do differently in my life?
What have I been putting off?
Why did I come here?
What do I wish to do?

710

Helping others is a shortcut to helping oneself. Be sure to take the steps available to you in both the directions of helping oneself and others.

~

711

In order to feel full,
be sure to feed another.

712

How can one expect to feel at peace in a
world that they do not quietly sit within?
Take time for self/ the All.

~

713

Challenges arise in order for things to shift.
Navigate with grace this realm that changes
in each moment, and you with it.

714

Look to the birds.
They write of the ways of the All.

~

715

Returning to source is a misconception.
We are all, always source. Like mini mobile
portals, you are each creating all of the time,
and, as one, we are the source. When you pass
you will become more tangibly at one
with the All. No thing has changed,
only your perception.

716

All creatures are 'God.'

~

717

You are all 'God.'

718

Express grace with precision by
doing precisely as you feel.

~

719

The trees are a part of you, the earth is a part
of you the All is all of you.

720

Breathe in the sky.
It is you.

~

721

Listening to oneself is
listening to God.

722

Treat others as you feel to, they are all the All.
If we mistreat another, we mistreat ourselves.

~

723

The Earth's crust is akin to your own skin.

724

Know your oneness with the All and be free.

~

725

You are not an extension on the All, you are
the All. We are not only connected,
we are all one.

726

By listening to yourself, you may create
at your optimum.

~

727

Step lightly, step intuitively, step accurately.
Feel all that is.

728

God is you.

~

729

Separation is an illusion.

730

Appreciate all things for you are all things.

~

731

Patience promotes peace.

732

Listen.

~

733

Your highest potential is cohesive
and conscious oneness. Each of us are
moving in the direction of this and none
can change this eventual destiny. As far off
track as you appear to be, know that we are
all transitioning as one. Do not fear being
left behind, or not doing as good a job at
contributing to this shift as another,
for it is a collective destiny
and all are one.

734

Your love and appreciation of that which
apparently surrounds you assists in co-creating
more of that which you love in this world.

~

735

Listening to your heart is both one
of the most simple and challenging things
to do. One can hear the truth when one
stops insisting one already knows.

736

The mind is a part of the All and the heart is
a part of the All. Both are equally important.
Both work best with the assistance
of the other.

~

737

Prioritize time to simply 'be.'

738

Being at one with the All is as simple as doing
what you feel.

~

739

We are each all of all that is.

740

Darkness is an illusion set in place to
catapult all into further expansion.

~

741

Nothing can stop the wholistic
expansion of all that is.

742

By taking the time to do as one feels,
one is changing all else in existence. Playing
your part in co-creating harmony is the most
efficient way of existing upon this plane,
or indeed any other.

~

743

Do not expect others to understand you.
Instead, seek to understand yourself.

744

Do not seek the validation of others. Instead assess your actions and make sure they are in alignment with your integral resonance.

~

745

Since all is changing all the time, the best thing to do in any moment is that which you feel, for that which you think may no longer be relevant.

746

Be kind to those whom surround you.
Co-creation works best when the inhabitants
are in the wisdom that they are one another.

~

747

Help one another along their course,
we will excel if assisting one another.

748

There is nothing to fear in this world and the
best way to feel stability and contentment
is by assisting others in finding such.

~

749

Listening to one's soul is as simple
as doing as one feels.

750

Listen to yourself for you are the All.

~

751

Behaving as you feel is
behaving in line with grace.

752

In each step you take, with each word you say,
be sure to step in grace.

~

753

Regarding another with any
less love than you have for oneself is
essentially disrespecting oneself.

754

That which surrounds you is not an illusion,
it is you. The only illusion is separation.
We are all one, and as one we are in balance.

~

755

That which you perceive is that which
you continue to create.

756

Be conscious of what you are creating in this
world; you are each creating all of the time.

~

757

Listening to yourself is the key to
hearing all else in existence.

758

All is sacred. Be kind and respectful to all.

~

759

Kindness brings peace to all involved.

760

Taking time for others is as important as
taking time for self. Each should be intuited
carefully. Balance found upon a personal level
meets balance found upon a terrestrial level,
and indeed this reflects unto all
else in existence.

~

761

None of you have 'a soul mate.' All of you
have many soul mates. For some that will
mean a lifetime of union, for others it will
mean a range of different experiences.
Do always as you feel and be kind
and respectful to all beings.

762

'Life' is a string of lessons you
write in collaboration for yourselves and
others. We are all changing all that is all the
time and there is nothing more important
than doing precisely as you feel.

~

763

Time doesn't exist and yet
'timing is everything.' The truth is,
from a place of presence all is possible,
and by navigating with grace one is able
to step in tune with the All. Alignments will
come into place which could not have were
you not stepping perfectly upon your path.
All happens in conjunction more accurately
when one steps most accurately. One can
only step accurately when in tune with
oneself and when being honest with
oneself about who they are.

764

Pay attention to all things for all
things are by your co-creation and hold
greatsignificance. You can determine most
future events by present presentations, though
all changes all the time and there is always
room for all to change.

~

765

Creatures, humans, places, and
experiences all come to one when
one is ready for them. If you long for
something other than that which you
already have, look to that which you have
to enrich your life further. Appreciation and
gratitude for that which you have will lend
to the accruing of more of that which you
need in your life. Ironically, the best way
to receive what you need in life is
to be happy with that which
you already have.

766

If you are miserable, make another smile.
If you are heartbroken, help to heal the heart
of another. If you are lonely, seek to comfort
another. Always ask oneself
'what have I to offer?'

~

767

You are each a miracle.
What is the particular miracle that is you?
Be unabashedly this being.
We all need you.

768

You may procrastinate for as many
lifetimes as you like but I highly recommend
to do precisely as you feel all of the time. This
is a masterful way in which to navigate the
world and will result in your own
exponential growth and
that of the All.

~

769

Nothing that you experience
is ever quite how you pictured it.
Why continue imagining that
this will be the case?

770

Create that which you wish for upon a soul
level by doing that which you feel
to upon a soul level.

~

771

Forgiveness is one of the most significant
gifts one can give. It is available to all of you
and has an immense capacity to
change the world.

772

If you are struggling to reach that which you
wish for, reach within yourself.

~

773

You are at the center of the Universe,
all the time. So are we all.

774

If you listen to yourself, you will hear the All.

~

775

Nourish your soul;
do as you feel.

776

By taking time for self, you are changing time.

~

777

By listening to the All you can find
your footing within the flow.

778

Immense wisdom comes to those
whom know their oneness with the All.

~

779

Forget you know anything and know you
know everything, as it is, as it changes,
all the 'time,' for you are the All.

780

Waiting for something to change is inefficient.
Instead, take the steps available to you so that
all may come into alignment. Remember,
the step available to you may not seem to
be in the direction you wish to travel.
Step intuitively and always do that
which you feel to upon
a soul level.

~

781

Listening to all that is, is as simple as doing as
you feel in each moment.

782

Wishing upon a star is one way
of putting your intentions out there,
taking the steps available is imperative to
'connecting the dots' so to speak. Ignore
these and your path will lengthen.

~

783

If you wish to be more 'successful' upon this
plane, ask yourself why it was you came here
and what you have to offer the All. You cannot
take physical possessions when you leave and
the greatest thing you may take with you is
the accomplishment of your quest.

784

Finish that which you feel to,
leaving things undone or uncompleted
can create a void which you can fall into.
Do always as you feel.

~

785

There is no simpler task upon this
plane than the one you feel to do upon a
soul level. Though this may seem challenging,
it is the very most smooth course to take
if you desire to upon a soul level.

786

Kindness and presence gifted unto
another aids all in existence.

~

787

Forgive those whom have harmed you,
else you are harming yourself.

788

Take the time to simply be.
Listen to yourself and respond by doing
as you feel.

~

789

Don't want to get up on a Monday
morning and go to work? Does this mean
there are significant steps available to you in
a different direction? Are there other means
by which you could support yourself? Does
your job feel like the right thing for you
to be doing in this moment or is there an
alternative waiting for you to embrace it?
Look for opportunities at your feet. You
may be ignoring a seemingly unrelated
first step in the direction
of your dreams.

790

By becoming that which you came here to be,
you co-form the multiverse as we, as a whole,
wish it to be. Your power is immense beyond
your personal perception.

~

791

We are living in a multi-dimensional reality
or 'multiverse.' That which you do
affects all else in existence.

792

Choose wisely your path upon this plane for
you chose to be here for perfect reason and
the smoothest path is paved by
steps taken intuitively.

~

793

Listening to the All is as simple
as doing as you feel.

794

God is everything. God is in the details.
There is no thing within which
you will not find God.

~

795

If you wish for your life to change,
make the changes life is asking of you.

796

Love everything for you are everything,
and so that which you condemn is also you.

~

797

You are a 'miracle.' You are all that is.
You are 'God' and so is all else in existence.
What shall we do? Choose consciously that
which you are co-creating. You are powerful
beyond perception upon this plane.

798

As your consciousness shifts,
so too does all in existence.

~

799

You can change the world by
changing your mind.

800

Everything that exists does so in accordance with everything else. Do not doubt the inter connectivity of all things, it is all that is.

~

801

Use your oneness with all that is.
Be all powerful.
Do as feels correct on a soul level.

802

Quiet your mind and find the
truth within yourself.

~

803

Placing your trust in 'God' is placing
your trust in self. Listen to yourself.
Listen to the signs around you. Listen to
that which you are a 'part' of. The All is in
constant conversation with itself in many
ways. The answers to all of life's mysteries
lie within life itself. Sometimes one must
step out to see in. Take the time and
space needed for perspective.

804

Wisdom comes to those who know
that they don't 'know.'

~

805

Teach only that which you feel,
not that which you think. You may limit
others with your own interpretations and
what you think may be relevant to your
path and bewildering for another's.

806

Perfection comes in many forms.
We are all perfect as one.

~

807

If you wish to leave this plane,
focus upon why it is you came.

808

Those who stand within their own light
are torches for all others.

~

809

Become that which you are by
simply being. You are not that which
you have been taught to be. You are the All,
in temporary form, expressing itself as
an apparent individual.

810

Discussions are sometimes enlightening and sometimes unhelpful. Be intuitive about when to speak. When to share one's 'thoughts' and when to be quiet. Humans speak far more than is necessary or 'helpful.'

~

811

Be kind to all beings for there is no one that you are not.

812

'Right now,' is always all that ever is.

~

813

By listening to yourself, you will find
it easy to step upon your course with
confidence and the guidance of the All.
Your challenges will become accessible to
you and your blessings will become
clearer and more common.

814

'Human' simply means 'hybrid.'
You are all hybrids.

~

815

The only way to expand is to stretch
beyond our comfort.

816

If a challenge seems so immense that you
don't believe you are capable of resolving it,
remember that you, in collaboration with the
All, created it and so must also have the
ability to navigate it with grace.

~

817

When another 'dies' or disappears and
one feels lost, remember that you are never
separate and that all will always come to be
in absolute harmony. We are all always
here and all is well despite the
illusion of separation.

818

Listen to yourself,
and the All will flow through you.

~

819

Take the time to simply be. It is within these
moments that one may behold the All.

820

You are now,
and have always been, everything that is.

~

821

Do not be afraid of anything for
you are everything.

822

Be careful to always do as you feel.
This is the way by which you can change
your world and all that is at large. Simple
steps lead to profound change.

~

823

Always take the step, or steps available to you.
These will lead you to the fulfillment of
your quest upon this plane.

824

Do not be distracted by others' challenges.
Assist them as intuited and stay in your own
vibrational field rather than to allow another
to disrupt you. This is always up to you.

~

825

Choose carefully the company
you keep. We are each absorbing energy
in every exchange and with conscious
participation one may choreograph with
precision that which is orchestrated
by the All at its highest or most
advanced capability.

826

Upon the breeze swim statements
of guidance for you all.
Listen.

~

827

Feel into the All. With every breath, with
every exchange. Know your oneness with
all that is.

828

Still your mind,
wisdom comes not in thought but in
knowing, in being,
in presence.

~

829

When you know you are the All you know
everything and nothing.

830

'Knowledge' can be a pathway to truth,
however, since all is changing all the time, one
is best suited to presence beyond presumption.

~

831

Taking care of yourself
includes taking care of others.

832

Be patient with one another.
You are all
'God.'

~

833

Kindness becomes contentment.
Patience brings peace.

834

Be yourself. Be all that is.

~

835

We are capable of removing the
constructs of reality which limit us for we
were the ones to put them there. We have the
ability to create whatever we wish to.
Our potential is ever expansive.

836

Nurture your body and your plane of
existence. Both are your being.

~

837

Dreams are another way by which to
experience reality. They are great teachers.
Be sure to listen to them.

838

If you ignore yourself, your greater self will take that which you ignore and gift you the opportunity of closer inspection.

~

839

The most effective way to complete your quest upon this plane is to do precisely as you feel.

840

Check in on others and check in on self.
Are we ok? Need we assist one another or
ourselves more greatly?

~

841

Forgive those who have harmed you
or else you will harm yourself.

842

Forgiveness is a way by which one may turn 'darkness' into 'light.'

~

843

Young children are closer to understanding this reality because they hold the perspective that this is only one reality and that we are not the individuals we came here to be.

844

Listen to children. Teach them not how to think, but how to think for themselves. Teach them not what to do, but to do as they feel.

~

845

Assist your children upon their quests. Do not assume you know what their quests are and always be supportive of their inspirations.

846

By taking time for self,
you are taking time for the All.

~

847

Without humans we could
not be at this stage of overall expansion.
You are a young being, in a sense, although
your energy has always existed. You have the
potential and the power to change everything
that is. You are in the process of understanding
your powers. When you do, the magnitude
of shifting within the All will be exponential.
You will one day learn that you hold all the
powers of the Universe if you submit to
them consciously and willingly. To truly
work with the All, one must
know their oneness.

848

All art brethren. All art All.

~

849

Life is what you choose it to be.

850

Listening to self is listening to All.

~

851

Behave as you feel to upon a soul level.

852

Listen to that which flows through you.
It is you.

~

853

Be aware of that which you are,
be aware of all that is.

854

Be kind to your brethren, for wronging
'another' is wronging yourself.

~

855

Welcome that which comes upon
your course. You must have chosen it for
good reason. If it is a 'problem,' welcome its
solution. If it is a clear blessing absorb it with
gratitude and appreciation. Know that all
that occurs in your life is by your
choice upon a soul level.

856

Define one's path by doing as one feels
to upon a soul level.

~

857

Be as the flower; grow toward the light
and blossom with all that you are.

858

If you are 'unhappy,'
bring happiness unto another.
If you are weak, find strength in that which
surrounds you. If you wish for your existence
to shift, take the steps that have been calling
you, as insignificant or unrelated as
they may seem to your overall
'happiness.'

~

859

Listen to yourself,
for you are 'God.'

860

There is no such thing as an individual.
You are all things.

~

861

Take the time to be in the moment, for time
does not exist, and you are creating all
that is in each moment.

862

Listen to the signs that surround you,
they were formed by your co-creation as
messages to yourself.

~

863

By taking care of yourself, you are taking
care of the All. Taking care of yourself means
doing that which you feel, which includes
doing much for 'others.'

864

Since we are all one, we are all affected by
every action, every thought, every event.
Be aware that by doing as you feel,
you are changing the world.

~

865

There have been many 'civilizations' upon
the plane. Some were more advanced than
yours, others were less so. You were all,
always a part of all that is.

866

Do not deny another your presence
for presumption of a lack of intellect.
You each have much to teach one another.

~

867

You are all, all that is. We are all, all that is.
All that is, is all there is.

868

Quiet your mind and flows
through you all that is.

~

869

Be immense.
Be all that is.

870

Know that you are equipped with all the
tools that you need in this moment
upon your quest.
Always.

~

871

Nothing can stop you doing what
you came unto this realm to
do except you.

872

The very best way to create life as you wish
it to be upon a soul level is to do as you feel
to upon a soul level. This simple truth is the
key to happiness and success upon this
plane and indeed all others.
Do as thy feel.

~

873

With each choice that you make, ask yourself,
'how does this feel?'

874

Nothing upon this plane is anyone's 'fault.'
We are the All, expressing itself in apparent
individual form. Blame not others, instead
find within yourself the light, the choices
and steps that are in grace, in harmony
with the All at its greatest potential
for wholistic expansion.

~

875

Trust yourself;
trust the All.

876

By experiencing that which
you came unto this plane to experience,
one is lending to the overall expansion of all
that is. You are each contributing greatly. Do
not doubt this. Despite challenges faced and
apparent failures, each being upon this plane is
giving most generously unto the All by simply
being. If you wish to contribute at your
optimum, simply do as you feel.

~

877

Do as you came here to do.
Do that which you feel upon a soul level.

878

Do not be disheartened. Instead, allow your
heart to grow to accommodate even more.

~

879

Listen. All that is speaks to you in
a thousand languages.

880

Be quiet. Be full.

~

881

Be extraordinary.
Be precisely whom you are.

882

You are everything that is,
do not question your ability.

~

883

Do not be saddened if
another does not 'love' you.
Instead, find greater ways by which
to love yourself.

884

The world is at a stage of extreme transition.
In order to stay on course, be astutely aware
of that which you feel. This will guide you
in each moment.

~

885

You came here to change the world.
You are the world, and all others.

886

Be kind, regardless of how others behave.
This will ensure that you and all others
will have the opportunity to
commune in harmony.

~

887

Do not be selfish for this serves no one;
not even you.

888

You each have an opportunity.
You each have a step to take.
Do you know what this is?

~

889

We are each here for a period of time
unknown. Be sure to do your will upon this
plane. There is no time to do that which
you do not feel to upon a soul level.

890

That which you are is reflected in all else that
is, we are all one and we are all in transition.
Do not be afraid of the changes.

~

891

Measure that which you value in
grace and gratitude.

892

Live as if you will not see another day,
hold no regrets and be kind to all beings.

~

893

Listen to that which resonates upon a soul
level, feel the difference between
truth and illusion.

894

You create all that is.
Do so with grace.

~

895

With persistence and precision,
one will find they are in a world
consciously created by themselves and
others. Do not lose track of your soul's
guidance, it is always there for you
and will always lead you
to your destination.

896

You are here to change the world.
In which ways do you feel it must change?

~

897

Know you have the ability
to do that which you came here to do.
Were this not the case you would not be here.

898

Since this Earth is your current
chosen home, be sure to take care of it
as if it were your own. It does not only
belong to you, it is you, the greater you,
and you cannot fully thrive without
you nurturing it as your own.

~

899

Question everything, not with your mind
but with your heart, your soul,
your true resonance.

900

Do not be afraid of others, they are you in extension. Instead, be aware of that which you hold within you and transform it into your highest integrity.

~

901

Surround yourself with those whom reflect that which you give unto the world. If your kindness is not reflected with such, be sure to find alternate surroundings.

902

Listen to your soul,
what is your calling – in this moment,
in every moment.

~

903

By listening to self, one hears the All.

904

Do not be afraid of fear.
Instead, ask yourself what you have
to learn from the situation, or in which ways
you might become stronger, more light filled,
more precise upon your path.

~

905

Do not allow another's perception of
reality to disturb your own.

906

By listening to yourself, you may conceive
of the fact that you are all that is.

~

907

One will come across
many beings, many places and many
experiences upon this plane. Bring with you
your inner judgement to each experience,
each meeting, each exploration. Within you
lies a richness of all that is, an inner light that
will show you which step to take in
any given moment.

908

Gratitude is a gift to the giver.

~

909

Every step upon this plane is a blessing.
As challenging as things become, be sure to
be in gratitude for your experience here, for
you chose to come and you create the world
you wish by being in this state of mind.

910

There is nothing more important
than doing as you feel.

~

911

Look for the gifts and the signs life is studded
with. As challenging as life may be, there are
always these jewels to be found
upon one's path.

912

Be sure to be kind to others even if you are
hurting. By gifting kindness unto others,
one breeds such an environment
for self and for All.

~

913

There is nothing more important
to do than that which you import to do.
What flows through you. What is your unique
gift? How does one wish to contribute to
the co-creation of the All?

914

You will always have all you need
for all you came here to learn and to
contribute. In any moment what is most
helpful to the All will be taking place,
for your own personal learning is of
great contribution to the All.

~

915

Do not be put off by challenges, instead
look to see what gifts they include.

916

Many beings need to experience
extreme challenges before they are able to
experience and bestow peace unto others.
Remember we are all in a state of transition,
all of this is temporary, and in each moment
we are all co-creating a new realm, precisely
designed as we, at large, wish it to be.

~

917

There is no one and no thing that is 'evil.'
There exists darkness but none that cannot
be brought unto the light.

918

There is nothing to be afraid of.
All in this realm and elsewhere was designed
for growth, learning, expansion. Instead of
fearing the unknown or that which challenges
one, position yourself within your greatest
integrity and look directly into the eyes of
that which you fear; knowing you are the
All and that you wish for the
peace of the All.

~

919

By simply listening to oneself,
one has the capacity to shift
the entire Universe.

920

Precision of path leads to accuracy of 'form.'
Create the world you wish to
by stepping intuitively.

~

921

Listening to self is
listening to the All.

922

Living upon this plane was a choice.
It has always been a choice. What do you
wish to do while you are 'here?'

~

923

Do not despair; find your footing in
what feels integral. Be present where you are.
Step intuitively, taking as much time as you
feel to upon a soul level.

924

Healing the world begins with healing 'self.'

~

925

You each have a quest and
we are co-forming all realities. You are very
powerful. What do you wish to create?
That which serves you, serves the All.
Each are synonymous.

926

There are a thousand ways
by which you may contribute
to the All. By stepping intuitively,
you are creating a brand-new path
made of possibilities created by
you and those before you.

~

927

What do you wish to do with
your apparent time?

928

You will find that as you take the time
to do as you feel, time and 'space'
will alter in support of you.

~

929

Signs surround you in each moment,
helping to direct one upon one's
own chosen path. We are co-forming
it with reality at all times. You choose
what reality is.

930

Navigate with grace; do as you feel.

~

931

Everything is conscious.
Everything is a 'part' of you.

932

We are all 'parts' of the same whole.

~

933

There is no such thing as anything.

934

Listening to self is the same as listening to the
All for you are all the All.

~

935

Becoming one with brethren is
as simple as breathing in.

936

We are all, without exception, all that is.
As one we can achieve unfathomable feats.
As one we are authentically ourselves.

~

937

Do not question your ability to do
what it is you came unto this planet to do.
You were designed for the task at hand, or it
was designed for your hand to accomplish.

938

Assist others upon their course and
you will find that your own is
more smoothly paved.

~

939

This 'world' only exists
because you exist within it.

940

Surround yourself with that which brings you
joy and comfort and do your best to provide
these gifts unto others. You are creating
the path that you tread.

~

941

Do not despair, simply look to the steps
available to you with a fresh eye and see
what opportunities are in your midst.

942

Become one with that which you oppose.
There is nothing you are not.

~

943

Be kind to others, even if they are unkind
to you. Listen to self/ All. One will not find
satisfaction in retaliation.

944

In order to see,
one must have an open
heart as well as open eyes.

~

945

Do not abandon nor admonish
another for the stage at which they
are upon their path. Instead, encourage
them and light their way by finding
your footing upon your own with
accuracy and grace.

946

Kindness unto others is kindness unto self.

~

947

Relinquish the temptation to put to shame
another, instead show them ways by which
they can come to the light by
being in your own light.

948

Happiness comes to those who gift
happiness unto others.

~

949

Take time to worship.
Worship is simply appreciating the All.
This is the same thing as
'gratitude.'

950

Friends are those whom love you even when you are not at your best. Be sure to surround yourself with such beings.

~

951

Take the time to distinguish the difference between that which you feel and that which you think.

952

Be as the plants; grow toward the light.

~

953

Listen to the birds, they speak of
the wholeness of all things.

954

Fear nothing, for all is in aid of you.

~

955

Do always as you feel and never
what you think.

956

Strength comes to those whose work
does not end when they begin to
think of stopping.

~

957

Bypass the mind and find stillness
within the All.

958

Know all by knowing your oneness within it.

~

959

Light is more spectacular when
it shines through the clouds.

960

Oneness comes to those whom are not
looking for it outside of themselves.
You are all things.

~

961

When one truly understands,
they will know that they are everything
and nothing. There is nothing that you are
not and solidly is merely a perception.

.

962

Since solidly is a sensual interpretation,
you may alter your perception and
experience it differently.

~

963

Be as the flower.
Open yourself toward the light and
display all your beauty unto the All.

964

Remember you are not separate and
so are never truly alone.

~

965

There is nothing that you are not.
Respect all things.

966

Do only, ever, that which feels correct
for you and the All.

~

967

Live in accordance with your soul's calling.
Ignore what others do, or expect from you,
unless these are in line with your own inner
callings. Raise the vibration of this plane,
and all others, by doing that which
you feel to upon a soul level.

968

Self is All. All is self.

~

969

Taking care of your greater environment
is taking care of self.

970

Listen to the All and know that you are one.

~

971

Listen to self beyond mind.

972

Listening to self
becomes listening to the whole.

~

973

Nothing upon this plane exists without you.
You are a part of all that is,
and you are all that is.

974

By doing as you feel to upon a
soul level you will be able to achieve your
quest, your reason for being.

~

975

Consider your work done upon this
plane when you pass. Know that each step
you take, each decision you make,
affects all else in existence.

976

Take the time it takes to listen to yourself.
Do not shorthand yourself. That which you
wish for is of the utmost importance.

~

977

You designed your course;
if you don't like it, redesign it.

978

One way to discover what it is you feel to do
upon a soul level, is to simply ask yourself:
'How do I feel?'

~

979

If you have to force something, then perhaps
it is not the step to take in this moment.
Timing doesn't exist; alignment is everything.

980

Time and space are not 'real.'
The only thing that is real is us,
as one, always.

~

981

Know that you have not lost anything,
nor truly gained anything, for you
have always been all things.

982

There is nothing that you are not.

~

983

As a flower bursts into the light, be in
expression of the expansion of all things, be
the unique character of the All that you are.

984

Know that you will always be supported by
the All, for you are at one with it at all times,
and cannot be separate nor alone.

~

985

Taking the time to be present will save you
much apparent time.

986

Time does not exist. You do not exist as
an individual. All is all there is.

~

987

Becoming one with all that is, is as simple
as knowing your oneness with all things.

988

God is all that is.
You are all 'God.'

~

989

Listen to self, for you are all things
and hold within you the wisdom of the All.

990

Peace comes to those
whom provide it to others.

~

991

Rest assured that no one is ever truly alone.

992

Do as you feel; not as you think and not
as you are told, unless these are in
line with what you feel.

~

993

You are everything you wish yourself to be.

994

When one is still, one finds stillness
within oneself. When one finds stillness
within oneself, one reflects such unto
their apparent surroundings.

~

995

Listen to self for there is nothing you are not.

996

Listen to the world;
it speaks to you in your own tongue.

~

997

Nothing is mightier that an apparent
individual in the knowing that they
are one with all things.

998

You are now, and will always be, all that is.
Choose wisely what to do in this world.
You create it with every moment
of your existence.

~

999

There is nothing more important to do
than precisely as you feel.

1000

Taking the time to do as you feel
is acting in accordance with the All.
There is nothing more worthwhile
than this. This is why you are here.

ACKNOWLEDGMENTS

Thanks and heartfelt gratitude to all who have come together to make this publication possible.

To Michael, whose extraordinary grace and guidance has kept me in strength and on path. To my family for their love and support, especially to my mother, Terri Andon for her many hours spent proofreading these pages. To Langley Fox Hemingway for her wonderful cover art drawing. To Anthony Young for the layout. To Phillip Dixon for his inspiration and for the rare gift of his friendship.

Thank you in particular to Editor Hannah Bhuiya, who worked in intuitive flow with Morcott to shape these "Thousand Thoughts," pairing them for impact and clarity.

And finally, and always, to Morcott for their unwavering patience, compassion, and guidance in our essential Oneness.

I am so deeply grateful to you all, and to be on this journey with you.

~ The Oracle of Morcott

DISCLAIMER

Morcott wishes to proclaim that the eye
pictured upon the cover of this book is
not in support of 'The Illuminati' but to
support the illumination of all truth for all.

All belongs to all.

When All discovers that all is light,
all will be enlightened.

Our intentions are to illuminate
all that is, for the All.

For more information on A Thousand Thoughts Food for the Soul, the audiobook version, or for the latest channeled material from Morcott, please visit:

WWW.MORCOTTMATERIAL.COM

Made in the USA
Las Vegas, NV
28 December 2024

e9988ec7-400a-4141-abc5-616526d45b0bR05

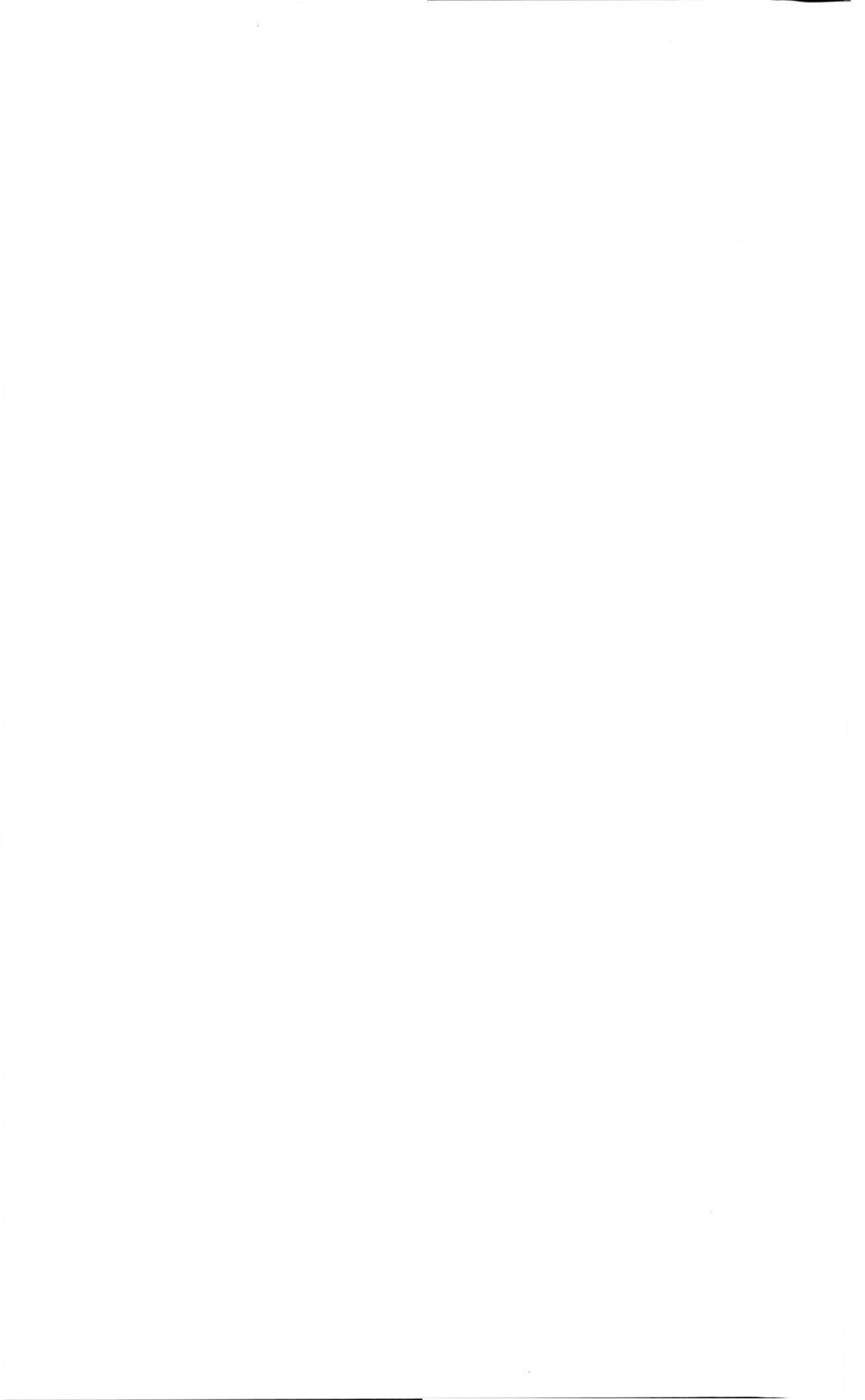